Exploring Architecture

BUILDINGS
MEANING
and **MAKING**

Exploring Architecture

BUILDINGS
MEANING
and **MAKING**

Eleanor Gawne
Michael Snodin

V&A Publications

V&A + RIBA
Architecture Partnership

For David
and
for Patricia

First published by V&A Publications, 2004
V&A Publications
160 Brompton Road
London SW3 1HW

Eleanor Gawne, Michael Snodin, Neil Bingham, Charles Hind, Tanishka Kachru,
David Lloyd Jones, Helen Thomas, Gareth Williams and Rob Wilson assert their
moral right to be identified as authors of this book

Designed by Janet James
Project management Geoff Barlow

ISBN 1 85177 435 1

Library of Congress control number 2004103253

Distributed in North America by Harry N. Abrams, Incorporated, New York

Front cover illustration: No. 30 St Mary Axe, London (Swiss Re Headquarters),
plate 1.3

Back cover illustration: Design for Broadleys, Cartmel, Lancashire, England,
plate 2.17

Frontispiece: Guggenheim Museum, Bilbao, Spain
Facing page: Concourse, Grand Central Station, New York City, USA, plate Intro.18
Preface illustration: Original front entrance doors to the Victoria and Albert
Museum, London, plate 2.55

Printed in Italy

**V&A + RIBA
Architecture Partnership**

V&A Publications
160 Brompton Road
London SW3 1HW
www.vam.ac.uk

Contents

PREFACE

This book has been published to coincide with the opening in November 2004 of the V&A + RIBA Architecture Gallery and RIBA Study Rooms for drawings and manuscripts at the Victoria and Albert Museum. The gallery, study rooms and this book have emerged from a partnership between two great institutions, the Victoria and Albert Museum and the Royal Institute of British Architects, working together to increase the understanding and enjoyment of architecture and the built environment.

The V&A has been linked to architecture since its foundation as the Museum of Manufactures in 1852. From the start architecture lay at the heart of the Museum's drive to promote good design in the applied arts. Today architecture is central to the Museum's mission to encourage the exploration and enjoyment of the designed world. The V&A holds one of the world's most wide-ranging architectural collections, running from drawings and photographs to whole rooms and other parts of buildings. From 1857 to the 1890s, these collections were shown in dedicated architectural galleries. From 1909, the architectural collections were scattered through new materials-based departments and displays. Only from the 1960s were the Museum's architectural riches again increasingly recognized.

The Royal Institute of British Architects' collections – consisting of books, journals, drawings, manuscripts, photographs, models and a variety of objects collected by, or of interest to, architects – were assembled from the Institute's foundation in 1834 onwards, and now form part of the RIBA British Architectural Library. The RIBA also collected casts and building stones, although later in the nineteenth century these were passed to other institutions owing to lack of space. From the outset, members of the Institute were encouraged to give the RIBA Library examples of their own work, or items they had collected themselves, to assist architectural students and fellow members. By 1971, the Drawings Collection had outgrown its accommodation in the RIBA headquarters in Portland Place and had moved to 21 Portman Square. Because the Portman Square lease was due to expire in 2002, the RIBA began to look for either alternative accommodation or a partner, in order to safeguard the future of the collections and make them more accessible. In due course, discussions with the V&A led to an offer of accommodation for the RIBA's Drawings and Manuscripts Collection in the Henry Cole Wing of the Museum. From this has developed the partnership that brings together two great architectural collections, complementing each other and creating at the V&A the world's most comprehensive architectural resource for both specialized and general audiences.

The V&A + RIBA Architecture Gallery is both international in scope and wide-ranging in date, from antiquity to the present day. Unlike most other permanent displays of architecture, however, the gallery is arranged thematically, rather than chronologically. It 'unpacks' buildings by looking at them in five distinct ways: the art of architecture, the function of buildings, architects and architecture, structures, and buildings in context. The arrangement of this book echoes that of the gallery but seeks to take the reader 'off site' to the wider world, providing more examples and exploring issues more deeply than the gallery is able to do. The writers and editors of the book have all been closely involved in the creation of the Gallery. It has been a truly collaborative exercise.

In making this book a reality, we have been fortunate in having had help from many individuals – including the staff of the RIBA British Architectural Library, particularly of the Drawings Collection led by Charles Hind – as well as all those at the V&A involved in the Architecture Gallery, led by Gareth Williams. Robert Elwall and Jonathan Makepeace of the RIBA Photographs Collection have been unstinting in providing illustrations from the photographs in their care. We would like to thank Nick Barnard, Kate Best, James Fowler, David Griffin, David Peyceré, Susan Palmer, Moshe Safdie, Mike Seaborne and Eva White for their help and advice on the illustrations; and Traci Young, Sara Sood-Kohli and Vanessa Roper-Evans for their enormous contribution in gathering the pictures from many sources. We are greatly indebted to Nick Barnard, David Brady, Tim Drewitt, Rupert Faulkner, John Guy, Maurice Howard, Greg Irvine, Tim Stanley and Ming Wilson for reading and commenting on drafts of the text. The design has been in the skilled hands of Janet James. Finally we would like to thank Mary Butler, Ariane Bankes, Frances Ambler, Nina Jacobson and Geoff Barlow from V&A Publications for their help in bringing the book to fruition.

Eleanor Gawne
Michael Snodin
November 2004

INTRODUCTION

Intro.1 Opera House, Sydney, Australia, 1957–73. Jørn Utzon.

Architecture touches everyone's life. We all live, work and play in buildings of one sort or another. Some make a big impression on us. They might have elegant rooms, a stunning staircase or breathtaking stained glass windows – all things that we love. Others make us depressed, especially if the escalator is broken, or there is so much glass that the rooms overheat. But it is only at these times that most of us stop to think about buildings: how they look, how they work and why they make us feel as we do. Do we mind less about getting overheated if it is in an impressive modern building, or freezing if in a beautiful medieval cathedral? Such questions about the precedence of practical over visual considerations, or vice versa, lie at the heart of thinking about buildings, and of this book.

Although we use buildings every day, we hardly ever really look at them. This is especially true of those we pass on our daily round. For many of us, even raising our eyes to look above door height is unusual. This may be partly because we find it difficult to be objective about buildings. We have personal prejudices, and a favourite style. We know what we like. Some of us may be inhibited by a lack of the technical language we imagine is required to talk about architecture. Most of us do not know how to 'read' a building, to unravel the signs that help us to understand why it looks the way it does.

This book aims to help the reader understand architecture in the widest sense. It provides ways of looking at buildings, so we can assess them more objectively. The more we understand buildings, the better we will be able to demand higher standards in our built environment. It can be difficult, if not impossible, for ordinary people to have a voice in determining their immediate surroundings. But this is what we should aspire to: no one deserves to live or work in ugly or broken-down buildings. All too often it is a small group of planners or architects who will decide what our homes look like or how they are used, or what the best use of some reclaimed land should be. Only by understanding buildings and the built environment better can we all have a voice.

Architecture is an enormous, all-encompassing subject and, although the book uses examples taken from many centuries and cultures, it is beyond its scope to be completely comprehensive. It is neither a complete history of architectural styles, nor is it just about landmark buildings. The book looks at ordinary buildings, like blocks of flats, as well as famous ones, like royal palaces, to help us understand them. Vernacular buildings are also included, made by local people using skills that have been handed down through generations and in which architects had no involvement.

Intro.2 Community consultation workshop, for the New Islington housing scheme, Manchester, England, 2002. Urban Splash and Alsop Architects.

The residents workshops were run at the Cob O'Coal on the Cardroom Estate, every four weeks. In between the architects visited every house to get responses to the scheme.

Unpacking architecture

Behind the creation of any building lie three basic questions: what building do we need, what form should it take, and what skills do we need to put it up? This truth was recognized as long ago as the first century CE when the Roman architect Vitruvius wrote that architecture was a combination of three factors – function, beauty and structure. This book seeks to explore and unpack architecture in the same way. The first chapter raises the question of function. In its most basic form, architecture is about shelter and protection. We all need buildings that keep us warm and dry, and protect us from the climate as well as from predators, both animal and human. But architecture is much more than simply putting up walls and a roof, enclosing space. It is also about creating structures that help us to carry out particular tasks, whether it is the worship of God or getting a good night's sleep. The second chapter looks at beauty, or the art of architecture. Many buildings are much more than merely functional. In fact architecture has been used throughout history to express humankind's deepest ideas and ideals. On a more personal level, we all feel connected with certain buildings, through their meaning and what they say to us. The third chapter examines structure, or the physical creation of buildings. Buildings are crucially affected by what they are made of and how they are constructed. Skyscrapers became possible only with the development of both the steel-frame structure and the lift. In some buildings this last factor is so dominant that we are hard put to decide whether they are works of architecture or engineering, or both.

Intro.3 The Crystal Palace, London – transept after the close of the Great Exhibition, 1851.

The iron-and-glass Crystal Palace was designed for the Great Exhibition by Sir Joseph Paxton. It was regarded by the contemporary critic John Ruskin as nothing more than an enormous greenhouse. The 20th-century modernist Le Corbusier saw it as the first true work of modern architecture. Photo: Benjamin Brecknell Turner, V&A: PH 1–1982.

Such questions show us that function, beauty and structure are mutually dependent. You cannot change one without affecting the other two. This is as true of parts of buildings as it is of complete structures. Windows need to provide light, insulation, ventilation and security, but they are also the 'eyes' of a building, playing a key role in the design of its façades. In complete buildings, like St Paul's Cathedral, the design was the outcome of a balance between the initial views of the architect, who sought a beautiful form, the practical needs of the clients and the type of construction. That the building combines them into seamless whole, a complete work of art, is a tribute to the skill of the architect (see pp.12–13).

Crucial to the design of St Paul's is its placing within the City of London. The fourth chapter looks at the siting of buildings, and especially at what happens to buildings when they come together in settlements large and small. Siting is the fourth great determining factor in the design of buildings. It affects design and materials but it also helps to determine the ways in which we perceive buildings. The Parthenon in Athens is carefully sited to make the maximum impact on the hill of the Acropolis. Seen side by side, buildings affect each other's appearance. Big buildings can be made to seem smaller than they really are and vice versa. We often take in groups of buildings as one, especially if they are built in the same style. The social and economic factors of settlements, including land prices and building regulations, have had a huge and often unnoticed effect on building design.

Art and architecture

Most buildings carry some sort of message and meaning. We have only to think about a home. A home is much more than a house. It is a familiar nest, a refuge, a personal place. It generates and reinforces deep feelings linked to our unique sense of self. How this happens tells us much about how the non-functional but meaningful aspects of architecture work. Imagine moving into a new home. At the start its rooms are echoing and empty. They have no meaning. Everything changes when we redecorate the rooms to our own taste and fill them with things arranged as we want. Some of these things and decorations will be highly

Intro.4 Chartres Cathedral above the town, 1194–1260.

RIBA Library Photographs Collection/Eric de Maré.

personal, such as souvenirs of family and friends. Others, more or less fashionable in design, will tend to reflect our social group and reinforce our links to the wider world. A home binds us closer to this wider world, as well as reinforcing the sense of unity of its inhabitants by creating and reinforcing habits and patterns of behaviour. It becomes associated with family and friends, with events, with sounds and even smells. At home, as in every building, all our senses are in play. But a home is not unchanging. It alters as some people leave and others get older. A home is a true physical reflection and expression of ourselves and our lives.

Public and official buildings also carry messages and meanings. Such buildings can, of course, mean something at a personal level: for many people an airport has exciting associations of travel, but for others it means the distress of parting. But most such buildings have been designed to give out certain clear messages. The huge bulk and massed spires of Gothic cathedrals dominated the low-built medieval towns in which they stood. These great churches were conceived in an age of faith, as symbols of immense spiritual and material power. Their soaring interiors, lit by enormous areas of coloured glass (at a time when glass was extremely rare), were designed for maximum spiritual effect: they created heaven on earth. Today, great Gothic churches still have a huge emotional impact, even though many of their religious and all their secular messages have been lost. Such buildings are works of art and demonstrations of the art of architecture.

St Paul's Cathedral

Charles Hind

The present building was born out of a disaster: the Great Fire that destroyed the City of London in September 1666, together with the great medieval cathedral that was one of the largest in Christendom. Old St Paul's had long been a source of embarrassment. In increasingly dangerous structural condition since the Reformation, the depredations it suffered during the Commonwealth in the 1650s led to a partial collapse that had not been repaired by the time of the Fire.

The task of designing its successor fell to the young mathematician and novice architect Christopher Wren, a member of the group of scientific scholars who later founded the Royal Society. Wren's earlier proposals for repairing St Paul's had been accepted a week before the Fire broke out. These were awkward designs, attempting to further classicise a Romanesque and Gothic structure over which Inigo Jones had thrown an unconvincing classical cloak in the 1630s. Wren now had the freedom to design a completely new church.

The present building (begun in 1675 and completed in 1711) is a brilliant compromise that grafts a domed classical structure onto a cruciform, Gothic plan designed to meet the needs of the clergy. Wren's first ideas, for a centralized domed church in the form of a Greek cross, were rejected as too continental and as being too closely based on Roman Catholic traditions developed since the Reformation. The clergy wished to emphasize the legitimacy of the Church of England as the true descendant of the early Church, freed from the corruption that had led to the Reformation. Consequently, they required a directional church with a nave proceeding to a choir, in the form of a Latin cross. They also wanted a choir that could be closed off to contain the smaller daily services, and lastly a cathedral that could be built in stages, for it was evident that money could be short.

To William Dunn, FRIBA
who first suggested the idea of showing the construction of St Paul's Cathedral by Isometric Projection, this drawing is inscribed by MERVYN EDMUND MACARTNEY, F.S.A. Surveyor to the Fabric — Measured and drawn by R.B. BROOK GREAVES in collaboration with W. GODFREY ALLEN. Valuable assistance has been rendered by Matthew Dawson FRIBA & E.J. Sidwell

Thus the basic form of the building was dictated by the traditional ceremonies that took place within it. The need to create a visually adequate dome to ride London's skyline essentially drove the design to its logical conclusion. A larger dome than Wren originally proposed would have overwhelmed the body of the church while providing engineering problems in how to keep it from collapsing. Wren solved the problem at a stroke, by running screen walls from end to end of the church, built upon the aisle walls. These gave the church the greater visual bulk necessary to support the larger dome, while allowing him to conceal the flying buttresses that gave it physical support.

Until the second half of the twentieth century the elegant bulk of St Paul's presided over the skyline of the City, attended by its satellite church spires. Most of these were also by Wren, who was keenly aware that his great church could only be seen close to or across the city's roofs from the river. Consequently the design of the church spires

Intro.5 Reproduction of an isometric projection drawing of 1923–8, showing the construction of the dome and crossing of St Paul's Cathedral. The drawing also shows the screen walls concealing the buttresses that help support the thrust of the dome.

The original drawing by R B Brooke. V&A: E 2208–1929

was a key part of his vision of how St Paul's should be seen. From the 1920s, and particularly from the 1960s onwards, the dominance of St Paul's was diminished as buildings grew ever higher, while several of Wren's spires were lost to demolition or bombing. The immediate context of the cathedral has also changed enormously since the Second World War, with buildings to the south being cleared away and the ground laid out for amenity purposes, while, to the north, successive massive building schemes continue to crowd the building.

In many ways St Paul's Cathedral is the architectural symbol of the City, but it also has a wider significance. Since the Middle Ages, St Paul's has been the scene of national celebrations, whether it be a solemn Te Deum to celebrate the defeat of the Spanish Armada in 1588 or the wedding of the Prince of Wales in 1982. It is also the scene of national mourning, such as the funerals of the Duke of Wellington (1852) or Sir Winston Churchill (1965). The famous image of the dome rising above the smoke of the burning City following a bombing raid in 1940 epitomizes the importance of the Cathedral in the national consciousness, an enduring symbol of permanence and survival in a changing world.

Intro.6 (above, left) St Paul's Cathedral from the north-west, about 1900.

Sir Christopher Wren's lower Order of his two-storey elevations for the cathedral corresponded to the roofline of the houses built round it after the Great Fire of 1666.

Intro.7 (above, right) St Paul's Cathedral from the south-east, showing its isolated setting following the wartime destruction of the buildings that once hugged it.

Intro.8 (left) St Paul's Cathedral during the Blitz, December 1940.

Intro.9 The Taj Mahal, Agra, India, 1630–53. It was built by Shah Jahan in memory of his wife.

Intro.10 Bicycle shed, the Hague, Holland, designed 1997–8. Zaerts & Jansma architecten.

What might be called the 'art value' of a building is usually taken to be a measure of its significance as architecture. In the past this led to a perception of a division between mere 'building' (e.g. a bicycle shed) and higher 'architecture' (e.g. a cathedral). A bicycle shed, it was argued, required little design effort to create and had a primarily practical purpose, while a cathedral was a higher form of design with carefully considered aesthetic effects and complex meanings. At first sight this might seem a reasonable viewpoint. We are more likely, after all, to travel across the globe to see Notre Dame or the Taj Mahal than to see a bicycle shed or a bus shelter. But in fact the differences are by no means clear-cut. Art value is a sliding scale; even bicycle sheds have on occasion been designed with care and attention to effect. The position of any building on this scale is determined by the culture from which it sprang, or from which it is viewed. In the West, up to the twentieth century, the most significant buildings, artistically speaking, tended to be public: churches in the Middle Ages or railway stations and town halls in the nineteenth century. Today they continue to be the symbols of their ages. But things are not always thus. Nowadays, some of the most significant buildings of the early part of the twentieth century are perceived to be the houses and housing developments that came out of the Modern Movement. This was by no means evident at the time, a period in which enormous amounts of money and creative ingenuity were being expended on buildings using other styles and design approaches. Asking ourselves what is the most significant architecture in today's world, the answer – at the time of writing at any rate – seems to lie with three very different types of building. The first, museums, perhaps reflects the increasing importance of these buildings as sites of spiritual and cultural memory in a period when religious buildings have lost much of their original meaning. It is also perhaps linked to the way in which cultural, sporting and leisure activities have increasingly replaced manufacturing as an economic generator in Western economies. In Daniel Libeskind's Jewish Museum in Berlin, the spaces themselves evoke in the visitor profound feelings linked to the Holocaust, in much the same way as religious buildings have raised emotions in the past. Another remarkable museum building, Frank Gehry's Guggenheim Museum at Bilbao, functions as a dynamic piece of architectural sculpture, revitalizing the heart of a decayed industrial city. Like many of the world's most famous buildings, such as the Sydney Opera House (see plate Intro.1) or the Eiffel Tower, it is both a structure and a visual metaphor for the city it represents. The second significant building type today is the so-called signature building: a structure that, by its distinctive appearance, is designed to speak out as the prestige home of a corporation in the jumble of tall buildings in today's commercial centres. Buildings in the final category, sustainable or eco-architecture, have a special meaning today, conveying ecological values through their forms as well as their materials.

The story of the art of architecture is the basis of architectural history, the systematic study of which began about 200 years ago. It is usually told

Intro.11 Jewish Museum, Berlin, 1989–99. Daniel Libeskind.

Intro.12 Guggenheim Museum, Bilbao, Spain, 1993–7. Frank Gehry.

RIBA Library Photographs Collection/Jo Newson.

Intro.13 *Comparative architecture*, **1834. Joseph Michael Gandy.**

Thirteen selected styles are compared. Watercolour.

as a tale of styles or 'looks' changing over time. At the start, it was seen as a progression from the primitive to the sophisticated, often expressed in terms of a 'family tree'. The detailed story was often seen in structural terms, with architecture developing from a wooden 'primitive hut' that bore a close resemblance to an ancient Greek temple (*see plate 2.43*). Another approach was to look at the story in functional terms, the forms and structures emerging from practical needs. A third way was to see changing styles as an expression of the shifting 'spirit of the age'. In fact style is made up of all these. But what drives style, and changes in style, is the search for a built form that has meaning.

Structure and architecture

The title of Mario Salvadori's book *Building – the Fight against Gravity* (1979) sums up the relationship between structures and the basic principles that govern them. All buildings are constrained by gravitational and other forces, which architects and builders have to work with. They cannot just decide to make an unusually shaped building if they have not worked out beforehand how it will stay up, how its components will fit together, and whether it will be safe for its users. The structures of spiral-shaped buildings, buildings held up on thin legs or buildings with walls that lean have all in theory been researched, tested and developed before the building is inhabited.

Architects and structural engineers do not work in a vacuum, but are influenced by prevailing technologies, materials and the structures of the day. Tents are one of the oldest structural ideas, yet are associated primarily with temporary structures. But when roofs are made of Teflon fabric supported on steel poles, the idea of the tent may be used for a number of permanent, high-tech buildings, from airports to supermarkets. Such design approaches can result in incredible feats of engineering and construction. The ultimate superstructures are often very high, such as skyscrapers, or very large, like sports stadia, or span great distances, like bridges.

We continually try to push technology to its limits, and demand ever-more-daring and architecturally sophisticated buildings. Such buildings are made up of a huge number of components that need to fit together exactly. This entails thousands upon thousands of design calculations. Where once we used pen and paper to solve mathematical conundrums, today computers make it possible to work out precise details of structures. Technical analyses, like working out the stresses of a structure, can also be measured this way. This allows architects to reduce the thickness of structural members. Worryingly, it also narrows the margin for error in actual construction.

But even when a building's design has been tested to withstand great forces, unforeseen man-made errors may lead to partial damage or catastrophic collapse. Not everything is predictable, especially if new construction methods or materials are not tested or understood properly beforehand. The Ronan Point disaster occurred in 1968, in which a 22-storey tower block in east London partially collapsed due to a relatively small gas explosion. It was found during an enquiry that bolts that attached panels to the frame of the building had been left out by the builders. Its collapse was due to human failure, to a misunderstanding of constructional details, rather than to an inherent flaw in the structure itself.

Of course, not everyone strives to use the most advanced structures or materials. In many cases, people are happy to follow successful historical precedents. For instance, the architect Sir John Soane used specially shaped hollow circular bricks, first invented in Roman times, for the arched roofs of the Bank of England in the early nineteenth century. They are lightweight and fireproof, and ideal for building arched forms. In other cases, old technologies are revived and sometimes combined with new materials.

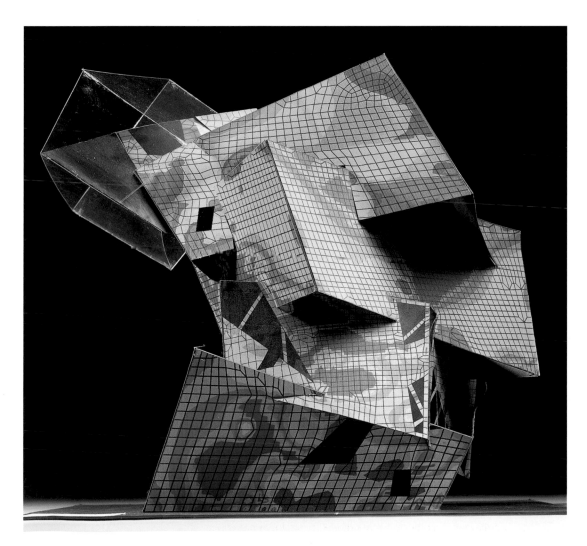

Intro.14 Structural analysis model of the Spiral Building, Victoria and Albert Museum, London, about 1997.

Designed by Daniel Libeskind and Cecil Balmond, model by Ove Arup and Partners. The red colouring indicates areas of potential weakness, the cooler colours areas of little or no stress. Card, perspex and computer print out.
V&A: AO 135(4).

NEW YORK CITY

Eleanor Gawne

Manhattan has the most famous skyline of any city in the world. The thousands of buildings that make up this great metropolis reflect the social and economic conditions that created them. All buildings, alone or together, are better understood if seen in their context. But other factors too have affected the city's physical form, including the appearance of buildings, their function, and their methods of construction.

The island of Manhattan was originally settled by the Dutch in 1626. Situated in a key position with a natural harbour and between the Hudson and East Rivers, it became a prosperous trading port. The southern tip, where the port and fort were located, was settled first, and a wall was built on what is now Wall Street to defend the city from Native American attack. As the port prospered, the city expanded northwards. In 1811 a city plan based on a grid was laid down to control the sale and development of land. Based on rectangular plots of 30 metres by 280 metres, this grid, known as the Commissioners' Plan, has affected the city's form to the present day. Straight roads were regarded as vital for keeping the city's transport, and therefore its economy, moving. One of these, Park Avenue, was built over New York Central railroad lines north of the railway station, Grand Central; in the early twentieth century, it was lined with elegant apartments and hotels before office buildings took over in the post-war period.

By the late nineteenth century Manhattan Island had become the USA's financial and commercial capital. Any expanding company naturally sought to have its headquarters there, resulting in the rush of building taller office blocks. Industrialists and entrepreneurs flocked to the city to share in its success, building themselves large mansions to show off their status, many of them sited overlooking the only large open space on the island, Central Park.

The close grouping of very tall buildings, literally 'skyscrapers', on the confined island has given the city its unique identity. The demand for these came from the rise in land values, but the key to their success was the steel frame and the lift, allowing them to be built to any height. In the 1920s and '30s thousands of construction workers were employed to build the steel frames. In addition, a peculiarity of Manhattan's geography is that it is a huge piece of granite, which permits solid foundations for tall buildings. When tall buildings are grouped closely together, however, they can create a wind-tunnel effect and unpleasantly dark, shadowed streets. The need to allow daylight into the streets was quickly realized, and the

outlines of skyscrapers were soon controlled by building regulations. The 1916 zoning law especially influenced the use of the stepped or ziggurat outline that we see as characteristic today. Coinciding with the effects of the 1916 law, stylistic influences from Europe, the so-called Moderne style, led to the displacement of Gothic and classical styles as the norm for tall buildings. Many architects and corporations seized upon modern imagery, finding it more appropriate and forward-looking for their new buildings. One of the most innovative, the Chrysler Building (designed by the architect William Van Alen, 1930) was built for the Chrysler Motor Corporation. Rather than stone, the building's cladding used new materials like stainless steel and aluminium for its symbolic decoration – in the form of hub caps, streamlined fins and gargoyles fashioned like radiator-caps, all similar to those on Chrysler cars – and acted as a gigantic advertisement.

To be successful, all buildings have to function well and be designed specifically for a particular use. Skyscrapers were a practical success. The steel frame structure allowed for open-plan floors and large windows, with the lifts and services placed in the core of the building, as they did not have to be seen. Grand Central Terminal (Reed & Stem and Warren & Wetmore, 1903–13) was also primarily designed with function in mind. The architects cleverly linked its 67 tracks on two underground levels to the main concourse

and associated shops, restaurants and hotels, by an elaborate network of passageways and ramps. These allow for the flow of people at different times of the day. The vast concourse has an emotional quality, perfect for happy homecomings or sad farewells. Its dramatic interior makes it one of the memorable railway stations of the world.

Grand Central Terminal was beautifully restored and modernized in recent years, but not all buildings in New York are so lucky. Until the end of the twentieth century, the pace of change in the hectic city meant that many buildings had a short life. Some landmark buildings were even demolished (like Penn Station in 1964), simply because there was economic pressure on them to adapt to modern life.

Intro.15 (opposite, top) Aerial view of Park Avenue, New York City, USA, about 1960. Howard Sochurek.

V&A: E 1328–2003.

Intro.16 (opposite, bottom) *Lunchtime, top of Rockefeller Center*, New York City, USA, 1932. Fred Zinnemann.

The Rockefeller Center was designed by Reinhard & Hofmeister Corbett, Harrison & MacMurray, and built from 1930. V&A: E 1668–1989.

Intro.17 (above, left) The Chrysler Building, New York City, USA, 1930. William Van Alen.

Robert Elwall/RIBA Library Photographs Collection.

Intro.18 (above) *Concourse, Grand Central Station*, New York City, USA, 1932. Fred Zinnemann.

Grand Central Station was designed by Reed & Stem and Warren & Wetmore and built 1903–13. V&A: E 1665–1989.

Architects and architecture

For centuries, individuals skilled in design have been essential to the business of creating buildings. The first individual known to us was the priest Imhotep, the builder of the stepped pyramid at Sakkâra in Egypt, 4,800 years ago. In Europe, since the sixteenth century, specialists in building design have been called architects (although they are by no means responsible for the creation of all buildings). The architect makes a design in conjunction with the client, who says what kind of building is required, and decides how much it will cost. The architect then communicates these ideas through drawings, models and a written specification, which may all change as the design progresses. The architect's final product is a set of instructions to the builder, in writing and as contract drawings. Although such drawings, accurately carried out to scale, may at first sight seem to represent the building, in fact they use codes that have been developed over centuries by architects and their draughtsmen. These include colours, such as yellow for wood and blue for metal, as well as conventional ways of showing standard features such as staircases and openings for windows and doors.

Buildings are three-dimensional. To convey their appearance and dimensions on flat paper, architects draw the building in three ways: in plan, in elevation and in section. Taken together, plans, elevations and sections drawn to measurable scale are able to convey all that is needed to put up a building. A plan is a diagram of the layout of a building. It shows how the rooms and internal spaces relate to each other. A plan includes information on the sizes of the rooms and the locations of windows, staircases and other elements, right down to electrical sockets and other services. Thus an airport is planned quite differently from a house, as they serve different purposes.

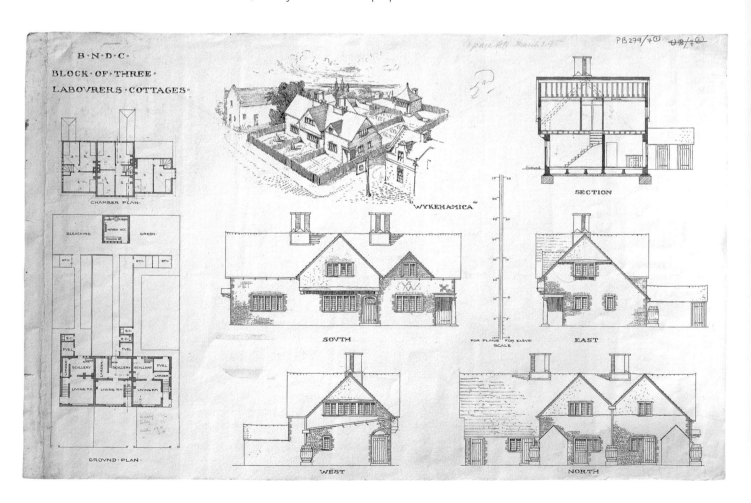

An elevation drawing shows what the outside of the building will look like viewed straight on, what its outline will be like, and how details of the façade like the windows and doors relate to each other. The architect will want to ensure that the façade conveys the right messages, that people will be able to 'read' the building from some distance. Although elevation drawings appear to show buildings as we would actually see them, this is not the case. When we stand directly in front of a building some parts are nearer to us than others: an elevation assumes that they are all the same distance away. In fact elevations are measurable diagrams, like plans.

Section drawings, which show a cut through a building, illustrate how the building will be constructed. They might show that certain materials are to be used for the foundations and others for the roof, whilst a particular structure is used for the walls.

While plans, elevations and sections are excellent for building construction, for most people they are a very unsatisfactory way of visualizing a completed building. For centuries three-dimensional models have been used to explain schemes to clients and to develop the trickier points of designs. Perspective drawings, showing the building in three dimensions, have also been made ever since perspective projection was invented in the fifteenth century. They are useful when the architect is working out his first ideas, as well as for selling an idea to a client or future occupier of a building. In the nineteenth and twentieth centuries, architects employed professional perspective artists to turn out enticing images for competitions and academy exhibitions.

Nowadays, computers are used for the entire design process. They are especially good at depicting the design in three dimensions, and for 'fly-throughs', which take the viewer on a virtual tour of the proposed building, showing the spatial effects. The client, or final user, may find these kinds of depictions especially effective.

Many of today's high-tech buildings could never have been designed or constructed without computers. Thinking about that helps us to understand and even admire the next giant addition to the skyline. But architecture does not need to be big and complicated to be enjoyed; it is often the simplest structures that affect us most profoundly. We hope this book will encourage you to open your eyes to look at buildings of all sorts, not just large and famous structures but smaller buildings like houses and shops which you might previously have overlooked. These also make up the story of architecture.

Intro.19 Design for a block of three labourers' cottages, competition design for the *Building News* designing club, 1895. Ethel Mary Charles.

The drawing shows plans, elevations, a section and a bird's-eye view. Pen and ink.
RIBA Library Drawings Collection.

CHAPTER ONE
BUILDING FOR FUNCTION
Michael Snodin

1.1 A cottage at Cherhill, Wiltshire, England, probably 17th century.

The walls are of stone, plastered. RIBA Library Photographs Collection/Edwin Smith.

A house without a roof is a ruin. It may be fascinating to contemplate, but it is useless as a structure – unless perhaps employed to catch the eye in a garden or landscape. Its very uselessness may give it poignancy and meaning, redolent of past glories, but it is no longer a house. Buildings are, above all, practical things. The earliest buildings were made as a protection from the vagaries of the climate. But their appearance soon began to take on meanings. In fact many of the meaningful features of buildings have a practical, climatic origin, influenced also by the use of local materials. The supremely practical pit houses of the Plateau Indians in North America, entered by a hole in the roof, embodied a cosmology based on the notion of the world as a house divided into four sectors, symbolized by the four roof beams. Such elements still contribute to our sense of place and of belonging, and to our basic human comforts in different climates: think of the thick protective thatched roof of an English country cottage or the cool calm arcades of a Sicilian marble cloister. Exactly the same practical needs apply today. Nature's rules do not change but we can overcome them, and we do so every day in ways we take for granted.

Buildings are usually made for specific purposes. They have to be devised and internally arranged in a manner that will work best. This is evident if we think of our homes and different ways of living. The numerous small rooms with specific functions of the British Victorian terrace house, for instance, fitted perfectly the social structures and servant economy of the nineteenth century. In the 1970s and '80s people knocked down Victorian walls to achieve the larger multi-purpose relaxed spaces they craved. Today they are trying to put the walls back. The outside stays the same, but the inside is very different. It is, in fact, the insides of buildings that most reflect their functions. But buildings have been changing their functions for centuries. The great mosque in Cordoba is now a cathedral, while the church of Hagia Sophia in Istanbul is now a mosque. In the West, economic changes (and powerful preservation movements) have meant that converting buildings from one function to another is now a major part of the work of architects. Things have also gone full circle, as new apartment buildings are built in imitation of warehouses converted to lofts.

Building and moving

The emphasis in architectural history on permanent buildings built of brick and stone has meant that movable structures of ancient origin, many of which are still in use by nomadic peoples, have not been part of the study of world architecture. In fact these structures have much to teach about the way in which climate, materials and the practical demands of ways of life affect the appearance and construction of buildings. The winter and summer shelters of hunter-gatherers and nomads need very different approaches from the permanent buildings needed for settled agriculture. Among the very earliest structures to be built were temporary shelters in the form of lean-to roofs built of a framework of sticks or branches covered with leaves or grass. This was a very important moment. For the first time people were able to create an environment separated from the rest of the world and to control the effects of nature. Two lean-to shelters put together formed a pitched roof and the first enclosed space or room. Walls probably appeared later: it was at first easier to get sufficient internal height (and less external exposure) by roofing over a hole or pit in the ground.

Structures made by people on the move in extreme climates are often sophisticated. Trellis tents, usually called yurts, are made by people following their herds across the central Asian steppe, with its hot dry summers and harsh winters. The yurt's circular wall is made of a flexible lattice of willow that collapses for transport, and its roof structure consists of long willow sticks. Both wall and roof are calculated to resist continuous strong winds. The whole is covered in many insulating layers of woollen felt secured with ropes

or textile straps. Lattice structures very similar to those of yurts are now to be found in so-called high-tech architecture. The tipi tent of the American Plains Indians is built of poles and buffalo hides capable of being packed up and drawn behind a horse, with no other equipment. Because of its large size, a tipi can accommodate a substantial fire in winter. The tipi is always put up with its back to the prevailing wind, encouraging smoke to escape from the hole at the top in winter and drawing cooling air through the tent in summer. The sail-like flaps beside the smoke hole can be adjusted from the ground if there is a change in wind direction or if the smoke hole has to be closed. The hole is also the main source of light.

1.2 A Russian Yurt, late nineteenth century.

1.3 No.30 St Mary Axe (Swiss Re Headquarters), London, 1997–2004. Foster and Partners.

Dome-shaped snow houses or igloos are the winter dwellings of the Inuit hunters of Greenland and northern Canada. They are built from inside using blocks of naturally packed snow laid in an ascending spiral, stuck together with loose snow. Only the tapering key block at the top is put in from the outside. After the blocks have been laid and the dome has been sealed, a lamp is lit in the interior to melt the snow, which is then allowed to refreeze as a skin of ice. Repeating this process eventually turns the igloo into a strong structure of solid ice. The low entrance is reached via a tunnel-vaulted passage, above which is a window of translucent ice or seal gut, illuminating the whole interior. The insulating quality of snow, together with heat from seal-oil lamps, can raise the temperature to two degrees above freezing, and even higher if the skin tent which is the Inuit's summer dwelling is hung inside. The igloo is a highly flexible form of building; several can be built together joined by tunnels, housing several family groups.

Staying comfortable

Human beings dislike extremes of temperature and humidity. In buildings we control these in three main ways: through the use of particular materials, by the design of the building and by using mechanical devices. The way they are used depends on the climatic circumstances. Thick mud-brick walls work well in the hot days and cooler nights of the Middle East, absorbing the sun's energy during the day and releasing it at night. In the same way, today's ecologically conscious buildings in the West use heat-retaining concrete floors to cut down energy consumption at night. The natural coolness of ceramic and marble – due to their high thermal capacity – means that in hot countries whole interiors are sheathed in those materials, cooling the air as it passes over them. Roofs in dry climates can be flat and made of porous materials like mud. The design and materials of roofing become especially important in climates with high precipitation, whether rain or snowfall.

Materials which act as a thermal barrier or insulation are useful in all climates, but especially in the northern hemisphere, where they keep the cold out and the heat in. Many forms of building

insulation rely on the principle of trapped air, like modern cold-weather clothing or the felt used in yurts. The porous softwood used in the log building tradition across the northern hemisphere is its own excellent insulation. In Scandinavia the gaps between the tightly fitting logs are filled with insulating moss. In more modern northern houses double (or even triple) glazing, with the inner panes being removable in the summer, also uses the principle of trapped air. Fired bricks, in use in China and the Near East since ancient times, and later used by the Romans, were only generally adopted in Europe towards the end of the Middle Ages. Used in a single layer, their high thermal mass gives them good insulative qualities – but this improves markedly if walls are built as two layers of brick with an air cavity between. Cavity walls also reduce damp and produce a stronger and more stable structure. From the sixteenth to the eighteenth century the relative drawbacks of single-brick walls were rectified by the installation of interior wooden panelling or cloth wall coverings. The insulating qualities of many of these traditional materials are today being rediscovered, sometimes in a highly visible form, as in the work of Sarah Wigglesworth and Jeremy Till with its use of walls of straw bales.

Roofs in wet climates have to get rid of rainwater quickly and must not leak. Unless a material can be put down in a continuous layer – like lead and copper and, more recently, asphalt and plastic – flat roofing is not an option. The horizontal top parapet of the typical eighteenth-century street in England in fact conceals a series of pitched roofs (often two to a building) covered in tiles or slates. Although the pitch or angle of roofing is not always related to climate, roofs generally get steeper as the climate gets wetter. Roofing materials reflect their local environment and society more closely than any other building component. Thatch made of plant leaves and stems has been used for roofing all over the world for millennia. Until 300 years ago most buildings in Britain were thatched. Thatch works by exploiting the tendency of rain to run down the water-repellent stems. A thatched roof, which has to be relatively thick to work properly, also has insulating qualities. The same is true of roofs in Scandinavia made of turf, resting on an inner layer of waterproof birch bark (also used in Native American canoes). Pitched roofs made of wooden or ceramic tiles, or pieces of stone or slate, all rely on the principle of overlapping units. Their construction is surprisingly loose, relying mainly on the weight of the material, as anyone whose roof has blown off in a gale will know. Corrugated iron, one of the world's most versatile and widespread building materials, is especially effective when used in large sheets on roofs. Water pouring off a roof must fall clear of the walls. Seventeenth- and eighteenth-century guttering and downpipes, made of valuable lead, were sufficient status symbols to be highly decorated, dated and marked with the initials of the house owners. Until the advent of cast iron in the nineteenth century many roofs were drained simply by having a sufficient overhang, the water being helped to reach the ground by hanging sticks or, in Japan, by chains.

1.4 House and office, London, 2001. Sarah Wigglesworth Architects.

RIBA Library Photographs Collection/Janet Hall.

1.5 Pipe head, 1698. Originally on a cottage, Bramhall, Cheshire, England.

The top of the pipe is in the fashionable tulip-shaped form. Cast lead. V&A: M.83–1921.

1.6 Openwork panel, *Jali*, probably made in Agra, India. 19th century.

Sandstone. V&A: IS 2–1993.

1.8 (opposite) Petronas towers, Kuala Lumpur, 1992–7. Cesar Pelli.

The overall shape of the towers reflects the forms of ancient temples, such as Angkor Wat.

Cooling down

In hot climates, the weather has had a fundamental impact on the local design language of buildings for thousands of years. The large overhanging roofs that are the hallmark of traditional Chinese building are a response to both strong sun and heavy rain. In Indonesian traditional architecture dramatically large roofs also dominate, made very steep in pitch to carry off the monsoon rains. It is only in the last half-century that mechanical devices have made it possible to put up in one climate buildings in a style only suited to another. Except for some local detailing there is little essential difference between a glass and steel skyscraper in temperate London or tropical Kuala Lumpur. This has been made possible by air-conditioning. Significantly, even in the West the same type of building often needs both air-conditioning and heating to cope with both the summer sun and winter heat loss through the large windows. Without air-conditioning other ways have been found to combat heat and strong sun, and the heavy rain and high humidity that often accompany them.

Once the building is properly covered it is necessary to exploit every passing breeze. Raising buildings off the ground is one solution – it is surprising how much more air movement there is even a short distance above the ground. At the same time it is necessary to keep the sun out as much as possible. The pierced screens on windows and balconies of the traditional architecture of South Asia and the Middle East have their modern counterparts in the cast concrete *brise soleil* of the twentieth-century modernist Le Corbusier, and in the metal light-shelves above the windows of office buildings today. The demands of Asian and African climates do not necessarily exclude buildings from other traditions. The colonial period in India saw the erection of a number of buildings in the Venetian Gothic style of northern Europe, including the university and main railway station in Bombay. According to the *Times of India*, the architect of the Victoria Railway Terminus, F W Stevens, had achieved in his designs 'with conspicuous success that blending of Venetian Gothic with Indian Saracenic by which he created a style of architecture so excellently suited to the climate and environment of Bombay'. Although these buildings may now seem rather out of place in an Indian context, the Gothic style is in fact surprisingly suited to a tropical climate, with its raised shady arcades, small window openings and large roofs. In the same way, the airy colonnades and covered walkways of the neo-classical style – a revival of ancient Greek and Roman forms – were also adaptable to a hot and humid climate, as architects in the southern states of the USA found. When Sir Edwin Lutyens and Sir Herbert Baker came to build the new capital of New Delhi, they combined the language of classical architecture with deeply shaded roof forms derived from the *chattri*, or pillared pavilion of indigenous Mogul buildings.

1.7 *Victoria Railway Terminus*, Bombay (Mumbai), India, 1878. Axel Herman Haig.

The station, designed by Frederick William Stevens, was built 1894–6. Watercolour.

1.9 Windtowers in Yazd, Iran.

RIBA Library Photographs
Collection/Bernard Cox.

**1.10 Menara Mesiniaga
Tower, Kuala Lumpur, 1992.
Ken Yeang.**

The traditional courtyard houses of Iran and the Persian Gulf are kept cool in several different ways. The thick mud walls have no exterior windows. A shady arcade in the courtyard prevents direct sunlight from entering the rooms. The flat roof, usual in an area of minimal rainfall, is a cool place to sleep at night. But there are also other cooling devices. Windscoops act like chimneys in reverse, catching and channelling moving air from roof level to the rooms below. As the air passes through the constricted passage it speeds up and cools down. Windtowers work in the same way but are higher and can collect air from four shafts facing in different directions. The shaft facing away from the wind takes hot air out of the room, exploiting the natural tendency of hot air to rise. Air drawn across the courtyard passes over the cooling waters of a fountain. In the same way the moving air can be passed through hanging wet cloths, which cool as the water evaporates. Some recent buildings in Asia have dealt with the challenges of a hot climate without using energy-consuming mechanical cooling. Ken Yeang's Menara Mesiniaga Tower in Kuala Lumpur has screened balconies designed to respond to the course of the sun and to maximize cross-ventilation, and a windscoop protecting a rooftop pool and garden.

Making heat

In temperate climates the demands are different but quite as difficult in their own way. Solid walls become vital as barriers between the cold outside and warm inside, and artificial heating a necessity – but not all the time. Methods of heating are certainly affected by cultural considerations and habit as well as by outside temperatures and available fuel. In Europe underfloor heating disappeared with the ancient Romans and was not to reappear until the nineteenth century. It has, however, always been common in China, where the whole floor of stamped earth was heated by stoke holes – life effectively took place on top of a stove. In Europe the central open hearth, in use since prehistoric times, was normal for most people until the sixteenth century. Even so, in some areas such as Scandinavia, poor country people continued into the nineteenth century to take advantage of the heat of their animals, living next door to them or even moving in with them in the winter. Wall fireplaces, for all their importance in the design of interiors, were extremely inefficient until the nineteenth century, most of the heat going up the chimney. The wood-burning tiled stove, invented in the sixteenth century, was far more effective; by the eighteenth century it had been developed into a sophisticated form in which the smoke and gasses were circulated round a series of pipes within the stove until all their heat had dissipated into the room. Chimneys, designed to draw smoke up and away from the fire, also had an important side effect as an effective form of room ventilation, pulling stale air out of the room.

The installation and positioning of heating apparatus has profoundly affected the design of buildings. The arrangement of chimney stacks and flues varies according to different building traditions. In many buildings, especially modest structures made of wood or earth, brick or stone stacks are the strongest element. For this and for economic and fire-safety reasons they are often grouped together in the centre of

1.11 *A dining parlour in a castle near Zurich*, **1643. Anonymous artist.**

The room is heated by a large tiled stove in the corner. Oil on panel. V&A: 6.A.63.

1.12 Villa Tugendhat, Brno, Czech Republic, 1929–30. Ludwig Mies van der Rohe.

the building, affecting the distribution of fireplaces or stoves and therefore the internal arrangement of rooms. In grander brick or stone buildings the arrangement of chimney stacks often reflects the need to have fireplaces as the centralized focal points of the longest walls of important rooms. The resulting chimneys, which need to rise above the roof-line to work properly, are hard to ignore. In the sixteenth century they were emphasized with a great show of rich decoration as a mark of wealth and modernity. But in other contexts they could be a problem. At Lord Burlington's villa in Chiswick (*see plate 2.44*), built in 1725, there was no precedent for the chimneys, needed in England but not on the Italian originals on which the villa was based. The results, curiously shaped as obelisks, are significantly omitted from the approved engravings of the villa. As houses and public buildings grew in size and complexity, the limitations imposed by a single source of heat in every room reached a crisis point. In Victorian town houses and office buildings a few stacks had to house a huge number of tortuously designed flues. Hot-air and hot-water-pipe heating allowed the creation of new types of building. The individual cells of the 400 inmates of Holloway prison in London, built in 1851, were heated by hot-water pipes laid in the corridor floors. The cell blocks were ventilated by air drawn through a central iron flue heated by a furnace. The introduction of hot-air and water heating was also a key development for the architects of the Modern Movement in the twentieth century. In Mies van der Rohe's Villa Tugendhat, built in 1929–30, the main living space on the first floor is a series of free-flowing areas centred on certain walls and groups of furniture. The open-plan space is made possible by a large electric turbine in the basement that sends both hot and cool air around the house.

Making openings

In a temperate climate openings in walls have to be very carefully considered. Ideally they need to be openable to any degree, and windows must let in as much light as possible. For centuries, with glass rare and expensive, this was a major challenge. Success was finally achieved with the sash window made of two vertically sliding units, which was invented in France in the seventeenth century at the moment that glass was starting to become more common. It provided a far better seal than wood-framed hinged casement windows and was infinitely adjustable. Buildings in temperate and northern climates need to exploit the sun for both light and warmth. Given a choice, rooms are made to face the optimum direction according to function. In English late-nineteenth-century country houses drawing rooms faced south, the most consistently sunny direction, morning rooms faced east while the kitchen, which must not overheat, faced the sunless north. In northern climates it is not uncommon for the cold north wall to have no windows at all. The early-twentieth-century realization of the beneficial effects of fresh air and sunlight, combined with the use of steel and concrete, made possible the maximizing of window area so that glazing could be virtually frameless between floor and ceiling. In the Villa Tugendhat's living room the very large steel-framed windows, which make up the entire south wall, disappear into the floor, opening up the whole side of the room to the air and view. The same impulse lay behind designs for houses with as many rooms as possible facing south, and even buildings that turned to follow the course of the sun. In modern office buildings, filled with heat-producing machinery and even hotter people, large windows that cannot be opened create problems of glare and overheating even in a temperate climate. These can be reduced by using 'smart' glass, which darkens as the light increases, and by installing light shelves – vanes on a projecting framework above the window, which control the summer sun and produce reflected light in winter.

1.13 Plan of the E.1027, Maison en bord de Mer, Roquebrune, France, 1929. Eileen Gray.

The plan shows the path of the sun, and its relation to the movements of the owner (as a solid line) and his housekeeper (as a dotted line). Pen and ink. V&A: AAD 1980/9/188/29.

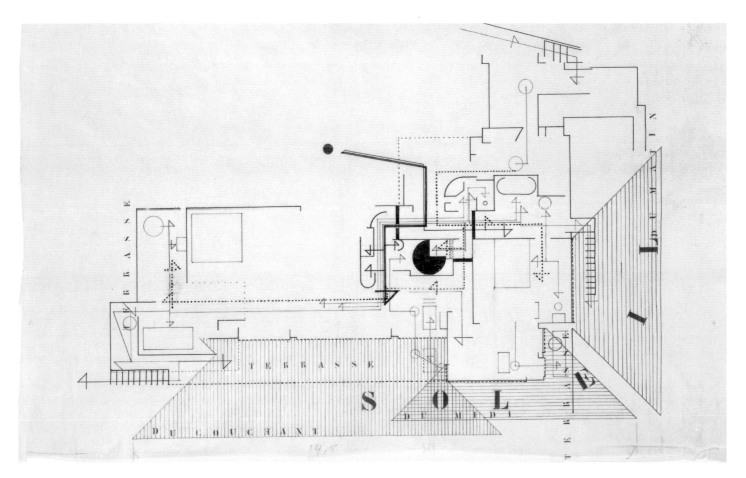

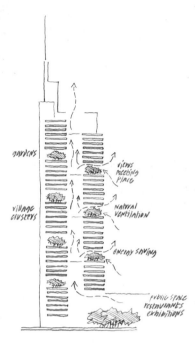

1.14 Diagram explaining the natural ventilation in the Commerzbank Headquarters, Frankfurt, Germany, 1991. Norman Foster.

Building for disaster

Buildings also have to face extreme conditions beyond those of climate. The demands of fireproofing have profoundly affected the design and material of buildings, especially where they are close together in cities. Up to about 150 years ago conflagrations were a regular occurrence in densely built-up areas. In 1631 the authorities in Massachusetts in the USA banned wooden chimneys and thatched roofs. In the City of London, following the Great Fire of 1666, a series of increasingly severe regulations profoundly changed the appearance of dwellings. Wooden houses were banned, as were roofs exposed to the street. Dividing walls had to be carried well above the roof-line of terraced houses, and window frames had to be concealed as far as possible in the walls. The search for fireproof building methods intensified as new types of large industrial and public building appeared at the end of the eighteenth century. The key lay in reducing the amount of wood. Beginning in England in the 1790s, fireproof floors were made of shallow arches of brick between iron beams. Although it was not at first realized, iron-framed buildings were not fireproof unless the iron was covered with some other material.

In many parts of the world earthquakes are an ever-present risk. Frame buildings survive earth movements better than load-bearing brick or masonry structures, but other measures are also possible. In Los Angeles, both the Getty Museum and the Roman Catholic Cathedral have concealed anti-earthquake measures. The Getty buildings actually rest on rollers, while the shelves in the library have restraining bars to stop the books falling out. The concrete basement of the cathedral, which is an official earthquake refuge, is placed on a number of enormous rubber pads and surrounded by a wide trench to allow for movement.

Sustainable architecture

Most new architecture today is to some extent sensitive to the problems of energy use in the modern world. At its broadest, sustainable architecture recognizes the energy used in making and transporting the building materials as well as providing energy-conscious design within the building itself. At its narrowest it means taking on a few ameliorating devices. The most complete design solutions combine age-old techniques of climate and comfort control with modern materials and technology. The BedZED housing and workspace scheme in south-west London is zero-energy. It is made of recyclable and renewable materials brought from within 35 miles of the building site. Water is recycled. A heat and power unit runs on tree waste. On the roof solar panels will provide power for the residents' future fleet of electric vehicles. The architecture itself makes and conserves heat and provides ventilation. The flats all face south, and have glazed-in conservatories to maximize heat. The north-facing fronts contain roof gardens and work spaces. Ventilating cowls on the roof, which swing with the wind, carry out warm foul air, at the same time heating drawn-in cold air. Temperature is controlled by adjusting windows and the ventilating

1.15 BedZED housing and workspaces, Wallington, Surrey, England, 1999–2001. Bill Dunster Architects.

chimneys. The 53-storey ecologically conceived Commerzbank in Frankfurt, by Foster and Partners, adapts for a temperate climate a number of the ideas pioneered in Ken Yeang's Malaysian office towers. Every office has windows opening into a central space that rises through the whole height of the structure, ventilating the building with its chimney effect. Energy consumption is half that of a conventional office tower. At intervals up the building are four-storey 'sky gardens' which bring daylight and fresh air into the atrium as well as providing a small-scale social focus for clusters of offices in this enormous building. Sustainable architecture aims to be good both for you and the environment.

SUSTAINABLE ARCHITECTURE

David Lloyd Jones

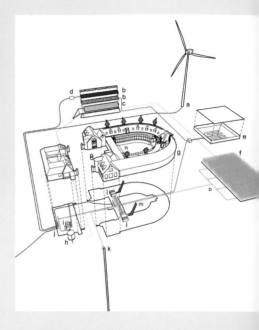

What does a sustainable building look like? Would you recognize one if you saw it? How is it sustainable? What is sustainability? The answer to these questions lies in the climate: social, economic and meteorological.

The contention that the earth is heating up at an alarming rate is borne out year-by-year by the incidence of increasingly extreme weather. Irreplaceable resources such as fresh water, coral reefs, rain forests, peat bogs and giant hardwood trees are being destroyed at immeasurable cost to humanity. Protection of the environment is now headline news. The concept of sustainable development has been conceived in an attempt to reinstate social, economic and environmental equilibrium. It may be summarized as: the dynamic process that enables all people to realize their potential and improve the quality of their lives, in ways that both protect and enhance Earth's life-support systems.

The construction and use of buildings, in the developed world, accounts for one half of all energy use. It is also a major contributor to the depletion of resources. The only chance of anywhere near meeting sustainable goals is to ally restraint in consumption with technological innovation. In constructing buildings, this means the skilled application of design. In fact, only designers are in a position to transform worthy, environmentally protective, palliative solutions into a celebration of a new ideal in which these counter-measures inspire a stimulating and regenerative built landscape.

Mass communications and unprecedented world-wide economic growth in the second half of the last century spawned an architecture that exists outside locality and region: International Style. This new architecture was appropriated by government, industry and big business. Denying its social roots in modernism, it now thrives – but only at great expense to the environment. To counter advancing disaster, designers must

rethink their approach. They have to both revisit traditional techniques and find new solutions.

So we now have eco-bioclimatic – sustainable – architecture, a movement without a satisfactory name. It is perhaps best to call it vital architecture: a life-affirming architecture for the affirmation of life. Unlike other architectural movements no recognizable style flows from its ideology. Sustainable buildings vary widely in appearance. Some choose to suppress visual evidence of their environmental credentials, others celebrate it with brise soleil, wind towers, thermal flues, grass roofs, arrays of

1.16 (below) The new entrance of the Renewable Energy System's Head Office and Visitors' Centre, King's Langley, Hertfordshire, England, built 1932, conversion and extension completed 2003. Studio E architects.

1.17 (above, right) The various energy systems serving the RES Head Office and Visitors' Centre.

Key to diagram

- **a.** 225kW wind turbine
- **b.** Hybrid photovoltaic/thermal array
- **c.** Biomass crop store
- **d.** Photovoltaic inverters
- **e.** 1500 m² seasonal ground heat store
- **f.** Biomass crop (miscanthus)
- **g.** The Renewable Energy Centre
- **h.** Biomass crop shredder
- **i.** Biomass boilers and gas fired backup boilers
- **j.** Electrical import/export meters
- **k.** 80m-deep ground water borehole
- **l.** Air-handling installations
- **m.** Fresh air
- **n.** Exhaust air
- **o.** Biomass crop irrigation

solar panels and the like. The best sustainable buildings, however, are recognizable. They have a certain poetry; a sense that they are at one with nature.

Fossil-fuel energy is the main cause of global warming. Measures for reducing its use are now well understood, and include: protecting the interiors of buildings from summer sun; insulating to prevent heat loss in winter; ensuring that daylight, and not artificial light, is used; ventilating the spaces naturally, instead of resorting to air-conditioning; and using renewable sources of energy. Finding ways of supporting local ecologies and conserving scarce resources is also vital. What has, so far, largely been ignored is the notion – implicit in the concept of sustainable development – that it not only saves the planet, but makes living on it more rewarding and enjoyable. In other words, it improves our lot socially, economically and spiritually. There is, of course, a limit to how far a single building can go in this respect. Nevertheless, it is the designer who is key. He or she can drive forward changes by example. Two of these are illustrated here: one already well known, the other just completed.

The Eden Project pursues the 'technical fix' approach to sustainability: doing more with less. Nicholas Grimshaw and Partners found an innovative structural solution – the form of which derives from the natural way soap bubbles combine together – that allowed abutted, fully-glazed, cost-effective, large-span enclosures. It utilized worked-out, derelict land, and has transformed the local economy.

The Renewable Energy Centre, a new head office and visitors' centre designed by Studio E Architects, also takes a derelict site but works with the existing structures (farm buildings built by Ovaltine to provide eggs for their malt drink) to convert and extend them for their new use. It is the first commercial, carbon-neutral building; that is greenhouse gases produced by its construction and use are more than offset by the savings in these gases made by using renewable sources of energy. By inno-vative renewable energy generation (electricity and heat from a solar array, a seasonal heat store, the cultivation and combustion of a biomass crop, a wind turbine and cooling system using water from subterranean aquifers), it provides all its own electricity and heat, and has some to spare for the rest of us.

1.18 (top) The Eden Project, St. Austell, Cornwall, England, 1996–2001. Nicholas Grimshaw and Partners. The two biome complexes nestling within the worked-out quarry.

1.19 (above) Interior of an Eden Project biome showing the junction of two domes.

Designing and function

The shapes that buildings take are very often determined by what they are for. This is very clear if we think of the great range of distinct building types that surround us. It is, for instance, immediately evident from the outside whether we are in front of a private house or a traditional theatre. Some of this recognition comes from the general size and shape of the building, some from the ornament or decoration (or lack of it) and some from characteristic forms like a prominent entrance. In fact these several visual elements have different origins. Some are functional, such as the clearly visible fly-tower over a theatre stage, others, like the decoration, have no practical basis, and some are both. The theatre's large sheltering entrance is not only highly practical but also symbolizes the building's public function. In the same way, the elegant dome and saucer on Oscar Niemeyer's parliamentary building in Brasilia at the same time symbolize and cover the two legislative chambers. The two towers behind contain the administrative offices.

At the Brasilia parliament the outside of the building shows the main internal arrangements. In many other buildings the arrangement of rooms and other spaces is hidden, but it is nearly always a vital element in the building's practical design. That is why the best way to start to understand a building is to look at its ground plan, even though it gives little suggestion of three-dimensional space. By looking at the room forms we can appreciate the function and hierarchy of different spaces. Some are essential to the building's function – it could not exist without them. Other, secondary, rooms serve the main spaces. In a traditional theatre the dressing rooms and offices appear as small spaces of similar size and format. The auditorium, a large room with a specialized technical function, is centrally placed and shaped unlike all the other spaces. The various lobbies and other areas for public circulation, which do not need to be a particular shape, are fitted in around the auditorium. A highly specialized building like a theatre shows very clearly the interaction between public and private space. At least half the building's volume is taken up by the stage,

its technical equipment, and dressing and service rooms. Of all this the public is blissfully unaware, as it progresses through a lavishly decorated lobby to an auditorium made to seem larger than it really is by the small spaces it has just passed through. Many other buildings have used such journeys through changing spaces for specific purposes. By 1700, visitors to the King, at the Palace of Versailles, had first to ascend the enormous Ambassadors' Staircase and then to pass through a line of connecting rooms that became ever smaller and more lavish, culminating in the state bedchamber. How far you got depended on how important you were. For the King to advance through the rooms towards you was a sign of the highest honour. Similar sequences can be found in corporate offices today.

1.20 The Senate and Congress building, Brasilia, 1957–60. Oscar Niemeyer.

Versailles relied for its effect and proper functioning on a symmetrical plan, with rooms for the Queen's household on one side and the King's on the other. But symmetry, so appropriate for formality and ceremonial occasions, can cause difficulties in other circumstances. The Casino, Sir William Chambers' jewel-like neo-classical pavilion in Dublin, has four identical sides which only partly match the ingeniously planned interior; two windows are half bricked up and the great front door conceals a much lower opening. Additive asymmetrical plans are of very ancient origin. In the pueblos of ancient North America single-room houses cluster together, sharing walls and gaining security. The Japanese imperial villa at Katsura, Kyoto, seems to be a group of linked buildings but is in fact a single structure made up of specialized rooms (*see plates 2.23 and 2.24*). The example of Japanese informal planning has had a profound influence on architecture in the West over the last hundred years.

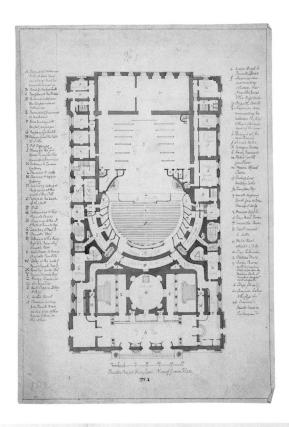

1.21 Ground plan of the Drury Lane Theatre, London, about 1813. Probably by James Winston.

It shows the theatre as built by Benjamin Dean Wyatt, 1811–12. Pen and ink and pencil. V&A: S 33–1984.

1.22 View of the Ambassadors' Staircase, Palace of Versailles, France, about 1720. Louis Surugue after J M Chevotot.

The staircase, begun in 1671, was designed and decorated by Louis Le Vau and Charles Le Brun. Engraving. V&A: E 93–1901.

Vue interieure du Grand Escalier de Versailles   *Prospectus interioris majorum Scallarum Versaliarum*

Staying safe

Security has historically been one of the chief purposes of a building after the need to cope with the climate. This is still true today, even though the means to achieve it are less evident. In cities from East Asia to North Africa, public buildings and houses have for many centuries been arranged around secure courtyards which present blank walls to the street, as they also did in ancient Rome. Within the encircling wall security measures are low. In Western cities a building tradition derived from the Italian Renaissance *palazzo* has resulted in street architecture in which the ground floor is blank or used for shops, with secure living accommodation above. Vulnerable windows were traditionally covered with iron grilles or wooden shutters. In British eighteenth-century houses the large and ever more lightly constructed glass windows were covered at night with internal wooden shutters strengthened with iron bars. By day these shutters were folded back to form elegant panelling. But danger can also come from within. In mosques, fear of assassination meant that raised and screened loggias for the local ruler were often a feature, sometimes reached by a closed-in passage from the palace.

The ingenious devices used in castles, the most impregnable buildings in a violent past, underwent a constant process of refinement as methods of attack changed. Castle sites were carefully chosen to exploit hills, rivers and other natural barriers. If none existed they were created, as moats or castle mounds. A series of walled enclosures of increasing strength led to the central dwelling or keep. At Himeji Castle in Japan the only approach to the main gate was up a walled twisting path full of blind corners and overlooked by arrow slits. Like the walls around a city or dwelling, a castle's gates and doors were as much for the control of the movement of people as for resisting attack.

Changes in military technology had a huge effect on the design of castles. The greatest was the introduction of the cannon in the fifteenth century, which made all existing castles – with their thin walls and tall round towers – instantly vulnerable to attack and impossible to defend. A solution was invented in Italy in the sixteenth century. A strikingly new type of fortification, as much earth as stone, it was designed in geometrical form to allow cannon to rake the whole surrounding area. The same type of geometrical fortifications was used to defend cities, and even found its way into Renaissance garden design and town planning. Today we still use many security devices, if less obviously than before. In both Europe and the United States security cameras have replaced the watchmen and gatehouses of the past. The US Embassy in Grosvenor Square, London, designed by Eero Saarinen, was built in 1956–9 with a dry moat around it. After riots in the 1970s the open area of the square was enclosed in thorny hedging, which performs the same function as the impregnable planting around many office developments. At the time of writing, following the events of 9/11, the building is isolated behind a row of concrete crash barriers.

1.23 Himeji Castle, Japan, about 1601–9.

1.24 Bodiam Castle, East Sussex, England, built 1385 onwards.

1.25 Charles Fort, County Cork, Ireland, built 1678. Probably designed by William Robinson.

At home

The design of our homes reflects perhaps more closely than any other type of building the society and culture we come from. Houses built for the small nuclear families of the industrialized West, made up of clusters of specialized rooms, are very different from those intended for the extended family groups that are more normal in other parts of the world. In the warm climate of Zimbabwe, Mashona families live largely outdoors in fenced compounds, which contain a number of huts for washing, cooking and sleeping. Like the different rooms in a Western house, the huts are allocated to particular family members, reflecting their status and social divisions. Similar arrangements can be found in the pre-industrial farmsteads of northern Sweden, where buildings having specialized functions were grouped together. In one example, now in the Skansen Museum in Stockholm, a whole separate building – strong, carefully locked and raised off the ground to protect it from vermin – was devoted to storing the family's most precious possessions, including its grain. The stable, cowshed and hayloft are individual buildings. The three-room main farmhouse has a multi-purpose living room, six metres square. The 'best room' was for special occasions, and the storage of food and special clothes and textiles, as well as for guests. Lack of space in the living room could mean that young girls slept in the cowshed all year, sharing the cows' heat and that of the fire used to cook their food. Washing, brewing and weaving could also take place in the cowshed.

In the Swedish farmstead the storehouse is more carefully and strongly built than the main dwelling. The whole family depended on its survival. Of all buildings our dwellings show most clearly what we consider to be important in our lives, their design making clear distinctions between significant and less significant functions. In the Swedish farmhouse many of the activities for which many of us now have separate rooms all took place in a single space, including eating, cooking, sleeping and daily chores. But it was a not a confused space. Even in such cramped conditions it was possible to create a sense of hierarchy, making clear which areas were more important. In some Swedish farmhouses these areas were marked out by a strikingly decorated pole hanging horizontally from the roof. In a similar way the great halls of medieval Europe were divided into spaces for the household and the lordly family. The lord's end of the hall was marked by a raised dais and the only window. The household both ate and slept in the hall, as did the lord's family at first. Even after a separate room, the solar, had been introduced for the lord's use, the raised end of the hall kept its higher status.

The story of the development of houses in the West between the Middle Ages and the end of the nineteenth century was one of a gradually increasing number of specialized rooms. Their place and arrangement tells us much about the societies and individuals that created them. The Escorial, the huge palace-monastery outside Madrid created from 1559 to 1584 by the emperor Philip II, is centred on its chapel. The emperor's small

1.26 The Älvros farm, Skansen Museum, Stockholm, 16th–19th centuries.

The storehouse is at the back on the left, the main living house directly ahead.

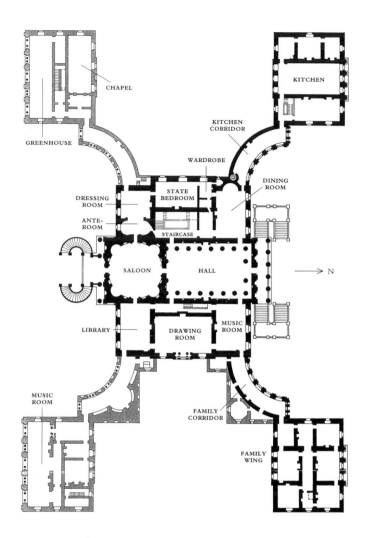

bedroom is positioned so that he could see the high altar from his bed through an internal window. Close to his room, stairs lead down to the Imperial vault. In eighteenth-century Britain the design of great country houses reflected very closely the changing ideas and priorities of the people that created them. Much more than places to live in, they were demonstrations of local and national political power. The imposing central block of Kedleston Hall in Derbyshire, built from the 1750s for Sir Nathaniel Curzon, contains a hall surrounded by a circuit of grand rooms, including a state bedroom. The whole central block was dedicated solely to entertainment. It is connected by curving corridors to two smaller house-like blocks, one of them for the family to live in and the other to contain the kitchen. The format of a centre with wings was derived from Andrea Palladio's villas near Venice, in which the wings served humble functions. At Kedleston the desire for symmetry meant that the kitchen was housed in great style. A hundred years later, the Victorian interest in rational and efficient design, the rejection of symmetrical planning and a strengthening of divisions between the classes and sexes combined to create house plans of great complexity. The ground floor of a very big house like Bear Wood contained nine reception rooms. Occupying an equally large but carefully separated area were 21 specialized rooms dedicated to serving a world based on entertainment and leisure, from brushing clothes to the storage of guns.

1.27 Ground floor plan of Kedleston Hall.

The two back wings on the left were planned but never built.

1.28 Kedleston Hall, Derbyshire, England, about 1759–65. Matthew Brettingham, James Paine and Robert Adam.

1.29 Bear Wood, Berkshire, England.

Illustration from *The Architect*, 9 July 1870. Lithograph. V&A: NAL PP21.D

1.30 Ground floor plan of Bear Wood, Berkshire, England, completed 1870. Robert Kerr.

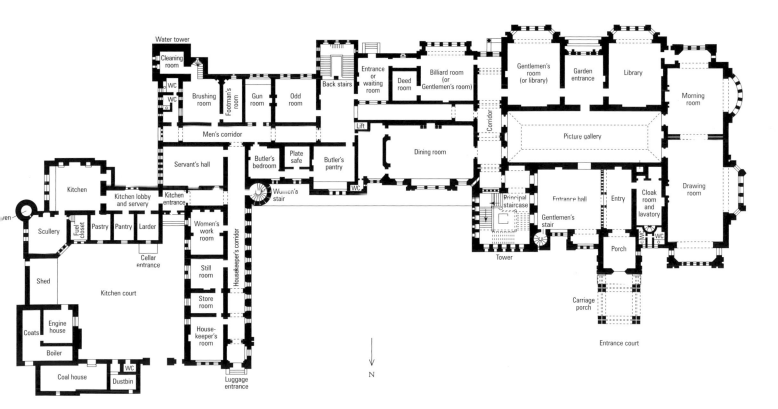

TRADITIONAL AND MODERN HOUSES

Helen Thomas

Does where we live affect how we live? This question has always been important to the designers of the houses we live in, but for many European architects during the first half of the twentieth century it was crucial. They believed that the cellular house plan traditional in Europe could not provide for modern ways of living. Every house has to meet the requirements of daily life. It offers places to sleep, bathe, cook, eat, sit in the evening and entertain on special occasions. As society responds to a changing world the balance between these requirements alters, and affects the rituals and expectations of each household. In traditional houses, separate rooms are given over to each household function. These rooms are organized within a vertical hierarchy. This arrangement reflects important distinctions between public and private life, as well as the relationships between served and servant spaces at the time they were built. With the coming of new household technologies during the twentieth century, these relationships changed.

In the typical British eighteenth-century town house, the kitchen and service spaces were sited on the ground floor or in the basement. The ground floor accommodated the entrance hall, private parlour and dining room. Grander public rooms for entertaining were on the first floor, as were the principal bedrooms. Less important bedrooms were on the second floor, with servants sleeping above. A decorative hierarchy reflected this spatial organization. The complexity of ornamentation diminished, along with room dimensions, the higher up the house you got. In rooms for entertaining, the taste of the owner was displayed in elaborate decorative schemes. The distinction between the public and private parts of the house were clearly delineated; the hall and staircase were both the public face of the house, but also the barrier to the private rooms that isolated each member of the household. A space dedicated to personal hygiene did not exist – there were few internal toilets and no bathrooms.

The American architect Frank Lloyd Wright was one of the first architects to challenge this vertical hierarchy. In his early twentieth-century Prairie Houses, boundaries between rooms, and between inside and outside space, were broken down. In Austria Adolf Loos challenged conventional house designs through his Raumplan, or plan of volumes. There were no simple floor plans. The character, volume and location of each room reflected the household activity it contained – it was as if all the different-sized rooms of a large country house had been packed together into a cube.

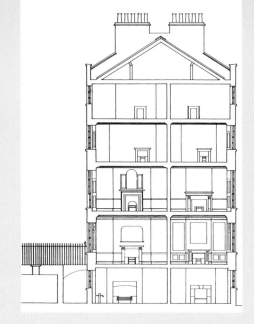

1.31 (left) Section cut through a typical five-storey 18th-century English townhouse.

1.32 (below) *Plan of a Room—shewing the proper distribution of the Furniture*, 1787. George Hepplewhite. Illustration from *The Cabinet Maker and Upholsterer's Guide.*

The furniture is that of a dining room, except for the pier tables between the windows, which would be substituted by dining tables drawn to the centre when in use. Engraving. V&A: 47 F 38.

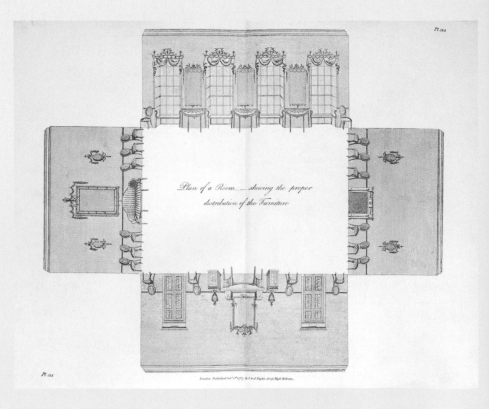

The French-Swiss architect Le Corbusier was the most famous architect to revise the house plan. His 'Five Points for a New Architecture', set out in 1926, suggested that a free plan should replace enclosed rooms. The open spaces of the free plan were achieved by separating structural columns from superfluous dividing walls. The Villa Savoye, 1928-31, epitomized the house as machine-for-living-in. Its flexible, open-plan spaces provided the light and airiness of the healthy modern house. A new kind of privacy associated with hygiene replaced the traditional public/private divide. Separate bathrooms and water closets became an essential feature of the modern house, as did the efficient kitchen.

Le Corbusier was influenced by the Schroeder House built in Utrecht in 1924 by Gerrit Rietveld. This was the first truly open-plan house, in which the whole living space could be either entirely open, or separated into up to six rooms by a series of sliding and folding screens. The house responded organically to the needs of its occupants as they changed throughout the day. Each space could be inhabited in many different ways, unlike the restrictive traditional house. It could be part of a greater whole for communal living, or closed into a private retreat defined by its furniture – piano, bath, divan – rather than a preconceived function.

In these modern homes, historical decorative traditions were replaced by a different aesthetic approach. Rietveld was influenced by the painter Piet Mondrian. Bright planes of colour expressed the structural elements of the building, and defined areas related to human dimensions and living requirements. Modern designers sought to free art from decoration and make it utilitarian and spatial. As in the traditional house, the plan and the decorative design of the modern home were intimately related – but these twentieth-century houses expressed quite different ideas about privacy, taste, hygiene and daily ritual.

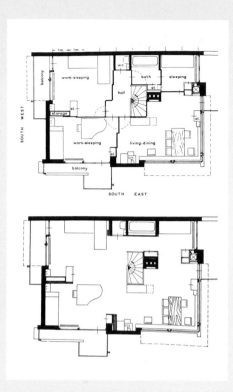

1.33 (above) Schroeder House, Utrecht, Holland, 1924. Gerrit Rietveld.

Upper floor plans showing the sliding and folding screens open and closed.

1.34 (left) Schroeder House. Open-plan upper floor living space, with a view of Mrs. Schroeder's bedroom, the stairwell/landing and the living – dining area.

The lines on the floor are tracks for the sliding and folding screens.

The limited spaces of city plots have taxed the ingenuity of house designers for centuries. In ancient Roman Pompeii, rooms around a series of open courts produced a relaxed inner world in marked contrast to the public life of the streets outside. In the terraced street houses of eighteenth-century British cities, architects and builders worked to fit increasing numbers of specialized rooms into plots that were at once both narrow-fronted and inconveniently long. Their basic model – of the stairs at the side with, on each floor, one or two rooms at the front and one at the back – had been invented in the previous century and was extremely practical. On special occasions it allowed guests to go straight upstairs to the main reception rooms, the family rooms being on the ground floor and the servants in the basement. In larger houses the servants had their own staircase hidden from view so that they were not seen by the master and his family. When passed down the social scale into the two-storey houses of Victorian times, these arrangements resulted in a ground floor that contained a dining room and best parlour, the latter a little-used temple to chilly formality. Most everyday life took place in the kitchen, although this was hardly acknowledged in its size. Today the number of specialized rooms has been heavily reduced, following a trend towards open planning, informality and an increased use of technology that has been growing since the late nineteenth century. The formal living room has largely lost its central importance, being often combined with the kitchen. In fact the most significant rooms in the house are now the kitchen and bathroom, as is shown by the amount of money spent on them. In the words of a contemporary interior designer: 'the kitchen is the hub of the household, the bathroom is where you relax. They're probably the most important rooms in your life.'

Ceremony and design

Buildings often serve the rituals and ceremonies that help to give structure and meaning to our lives. The front parlour of the Victorian home was a ritual space, used for guests and formal family events. Even when empty (which was most of the time) its ritual function made it a powerful symbol of respectability and family values. The British nineteenth-century courtroom was equally adapted to ritual and ceremony, its main actors clad in archaic robes and wigs and its parts strictly segregated. The raised judges' bench, marked by the Royal Arms, had its own door. At the court of St George's Hall in Liverpool, the prisoners' dock was entered up its own spiral staircase from a basement cell. Ascending those stairs today produces a strong feeling of being guilty unless proved innocent.

Of all buildings, those created to serve religion are the most affected by the demands of ritual and ceremony. They include the world's earliest major structures, the stepped ziggurats of Mesopotamia. Religious buildings are often designed to focus on processions and other ritual actions. The Great Stupa at Sanchi, in central India, is surrounded by a walled-in path for ritual encircling walks. The courtyard at the great mosque at Mecca can accommodate thousands of people all engaged in the ritual of circling the Ka'ba seven times. Religious buildings also frequently include segregated areas for real or symbolic sacrifice. Ancient Greek temples were dwellings of the gods that few could enter. In a similar way, the churches of medieval Christendom had a presbytery at the eastern end, separated from the main space, or nave, in the west. Their form was not a new invention, but derived from the ancient Roman public hall or basilica, used as a law court or place of assembly. In the presbytery the priests celebrated Mass at the altar, watched by the congregation separated by a screen. In Greek Orthodox churches today the congregation is still separated from the priests by a solid *inconostasis*, a screen of holy images. In addition to the main altar, larger medieval churches (especially those attached to monasteries) had many small side chapels positioned off the nave and often wrapping around the main altar in the east – many of them visible on the church's exterior. The numerous altars (there were 21 in Durham Cathedral) turned the church into an engine of almost continual worship, with Mass being celebrated many times a day. In medieval Catholic churches converted to Protestant worship, such as the British cathedrals – their side chapels filled with later

1.35 Crown Court,
St George's Hall, Liverpool,
England, 1840–54.
Charles Robert Cockerell.

1.36 San Apollinare in Classe,
Ravenna, Italy, about 534–49.

1.37 Interior of the prayer hall, the Sultanahmet Mosque, Istanbul, Turkey, 1609–16. Mehmed Aga.

The *mihrab* niche is in the centre, the *minbar* pulpit by it, and the *dikka* platform on the right.

1.38 Ground plan of Fountains Abbey, Yorkshire, England, begun 1140.

Fountains belonged to the Cistercian order. The lay brothers carried on the routine jobs of the abbey, leaving the monks to a life of prayer and meditation.

tombs and much of the colour and imagery removed – it is now hard to picture the way in which the buildings first functioned. A better idea of the multi-purpose nature of a medieval working church can be formed in the dark and dramatic spaces of a great Spanish cathedral, such as that at Toledo or Seville. Processions up the central aisle and Mass at the high altar are but one of these buildings' functions. Private prayer and worship also take place, as well as social meetings. The church, much of its floor clear of seating, is a major public place as well as a religious building.

The sixteenth-century switch from Catholic to Protestant forms of worship meant the removal of images and a new emphasis on the word. In English churches old and new the preaching pulpit and clerk's desk became a major element. When Sir Christopher Wren and his collaborators rebuilt 51 new churches in the fire-ravaged City of London, they recognized that something novel was needed. For Roman Catholics, Wren wrote, it may be enough to 'hear the murmur of the Mass and see the elevation of the Host' but the main requirement of the new Protestant churches was 'that all who are present can see and hear'. The resulting 'auditory' churches took the form of open halls, often with extra seating in galleries, even though the eastern altar end was still marked by extra decoration. A hundred years later the British Nonconformist chapel had developed into a bare but efficient preaching box, its east end dominated by the pulpit and clerks' desks.

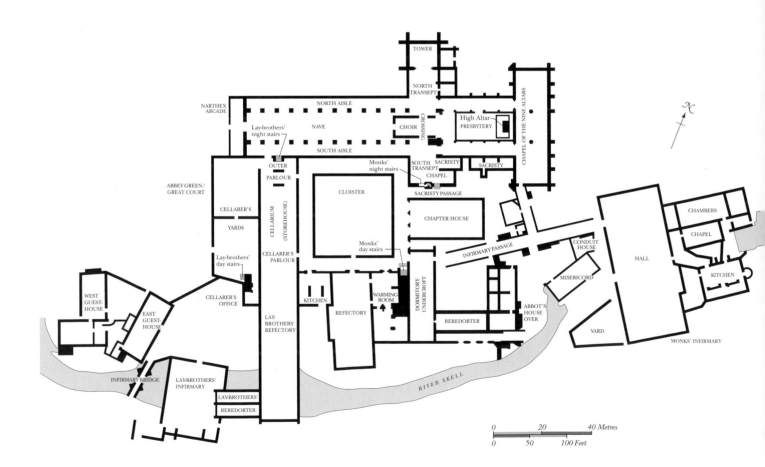

It is interesting to compare the function of these religious buildings with that of a mosque. The mosque hall is a place of preaching, prayer and meditation. Although there are regional variations in layout, all mosques have certain fixed elements. As in Wren's churches, seeing and hearing are all. Those praying face Mecca, its direction marked by the qibla wall in which is a niche or *mihrab*. The only other functional elements are the *minbar* or pulpit from which the imam makes the weekly oration and the *dikka*, an elevated platform from which responders repeat the imam's word to the congregation. The floor has to be an area large enough to accommodate the space of a prayer mat for each worshipper. In big mosques space also has to be made to take hundreds of pairs of worshippers' shoes, removed in the cleansing ritual. But a mosque is the centre of the community as well as a place of prayer. The prayer hall is often fronted by a large arcaded courtyard designed for resting travellers as well as sizeable congregations. Below the paving of the court there is often a large cistern for the fountains at which to carry out ritual ablutions. Around the mosque are schools and other social institutions.

A similar collection of community buildings was part of the public side of the Christian religious houses of the Middle Ages, which were major landowning corporations with charitable aims. But beyond the public outer court these religious complexes were carefully designed to serve the strictly timed daily round of prayer, work and study of comparatively small groups of monks or nuns. Attached to the church on its sunny south side was a quadrangular cloister, three of its sides formed by the buildings for sleeping, eating and storing food. This covered ground-floor walkway, which connected the buildings around an open space, was also used for study and reading. The cloister was additionally where the community could wash its hands before entering the frater, or dining hall. The whole community processed through the entire complex each Sunday never retracing its steps, passing through specially created doorways and finishing in the church, where everyone's position was marked in the pavement. Adapting to the rules of the community's order meant that there were variations in design. In Benedictine monasteries monks slept in cubicles in a long dormitory; in the stricter Carthusian order each monk lived in isolation in his cell with its own small garden, food being passed in through a hatch. The central open space of a Benedictine cloister was a piece of grass or a cultivated garden; for Carthusians it was their cemetery. The plain treatment of Cistercian architecture reflected that order's austere rule. The practical details of monastic architecture still surprise. A stair led directly from the dormitory to the church for early morning services, which began at 2.30 am. The monk in charge of timekeeping slept at the end of the dormitory closest to the clock in the transept of the church. Once in the church, misericord shelves on the back of the stall seats allowed monks to rest in a standing position. The solid wooden screen of the enclosed stalls went some way to cut out the draughts in an unheated building. The rule meant that there was only one heated space, the warming house, but there was a very modern lavatory, or reredorter, close to the dormitory, using water channelled from a stream.

1.39 The cloister, Gloucester Cathedral, Gloucestershire, England, 1351–77.

The Benedictine monks studied in recesses, or carrels, on the left.

Ways of planning

The way in which buildings are laid out can be divided into two types, both seen in the religious houses just discussed. The position of the reredorter, though placed as near as possible to the dormitory, was ultimately dependent on the location of the nearest stream. Even the buildings around the cloister, though often roughly symmetrical, were arranged as practical needs required. They are all examples of additive planning. The church, on the other hand, is symmetrically planned, its transepts of usually equal length on each side of the nave. As we have seen, this plan was more than merely efficient – its balanced formal design expressed and reinforced the rituals it contained. Many public and official buildings today work in the same way. Legislative buildings or parliaments are particularly good examples of this process in action. The Palace of Westminster in London (better known as the Houses of Parliament) is laid out along a 220-metre-long axis. At one end, where the monarch enters the building, are the Robing Room, Princes Chamber and Royal Gallery, while at the other end is the House of Commons. Between them is the House of Lords. They are all separated by lobbies. The whole plan perfectly symbolizes the workings of Britain's unwritten constitution

1.40 Ground floor plan of the Palace of Westminster, London, 1835–70. Sir Charles Barry and Augustus Welby Northmore Pugin.

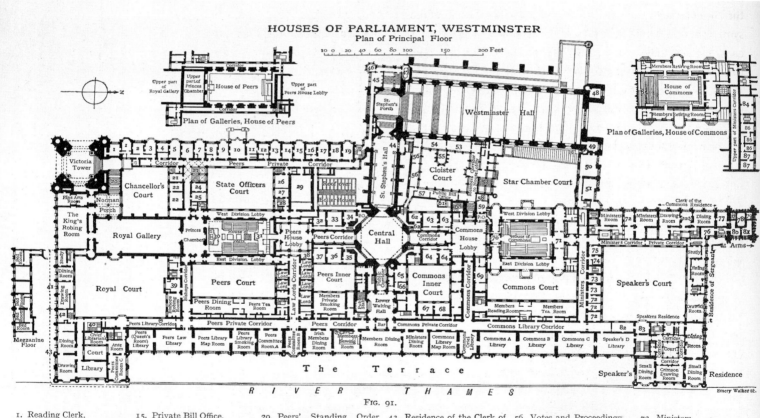

HOUSES OF PARLIAMENT, WESTMINSTER
Plan of Principal Floor

FIG. 91.

1. Reading Clerk.
2. Dressing Room.
3. Clerk of the Parliament.
4. Clerk Assistant's Dressing Room.
5. Clerk Assistant.
6. Clerk, House of Lords.
7. Messengers.
8. Waiting Room.
9. Lord Chancellor's Secretaries.
10. Lord Chancellor.
11. Lord Chancellor's Dressing Room.
12. Permanent Secretary.
13. Sergeant-at-Arms.
14. Yeoman Usher of the Black Rod.
15. Private Bill Office.
16. Chairman's Dressing Room.
17. Chairman of Committees.
18. Clerk to Private Bill and Taxing Office. [Counsel.
19. Chairman of Committee's
20. Royal Staircase.
21. Clerk to Public Bills.
22. Minutes.
23. Peers' Staircase.
24. Inner Office.
25. Printed Papers Office.
26. Private Bills and Taxing Office.
27. Earl Marshal.
28. Strangers' and Reporters' Stairs.
29. Peers' Standing Order Committee Room.
30. The Thrones.
31. Bar of the House.
32. Leader of the Opposition in the House of Lords.
33. Premier.
34. Telegraph.
35. Solicitor-General.
36. Attorney-General.
37. Lord Advocate.
38. Resident Superintendent.
39. Archbishops.
40. Principal Stairs.
41. Residence of the Yeoman Usher of the Black Rod.
42. Sitting Room.
43. Residence of the Clerk of Parliament.
44. Members' Entrance.
45. Dining Room of the Deputy Sergeant-at-Arms.
46. Turret Room.
47. Private Stairs of the Deputy Sergeant-at-Arms.
48. Journal Office Stores.
49. Police.
50. Ministers.
51. Opposition Ministers.
52. Members' Entrance Stairs.
53. Members' Conference Room. [taries.
54. Members' Private Secre-
55. Members' Small Conference Room.
56. Votes and Proceedings.
57. Accountant and Chief Public Bill Office.
58. Old Treasury Stairs.
59. Post Master.
60. Strangers' Stairs.
61. Cistern Tower.
62. Irish Whips.
63. Government Whips.
64. Opposition Whips.
65. Deputy Sergeant-at-Arms.
66. Clerk to Deputy Sergeant-at-Arms.
67. Speaker's Counsel.
68. Speaker's Counsel's Clerk.
69. Vote Office.
70. Bar Lobby.
71. Speaker's Lobby.
72. Ministers.
73. Clerk Assistant.
74. Train Bearers.
75. Speaker's Retiring Room.
76. Old Prison Rooms Lobby.
77. Sergeant-at-Arms' Smoking Room.
78. Clock Weight Shaft.
79. Air Shaft.
80. Smoking Room Lobby.
81. Butler.
82. Speaker's Secretary.
83. Audience Room.
84. *Times* Reporters.
85. Strangers' Gallery.
86. Waste Paper.
87. Mess.

as well as Britain's social hierarchy. The Commons process to the Lords by command to hear the monarch's speech before parliament. The monarch cannot enter the Commons unless by invitation. Within the Commons chamber the government benches face those of the other political parties. This arrangement, which imitates that of the converted medieval chapel the Commons occupied up to 1834, perfectly expresses and perhaps even reinforces the oppositional nature of British politics. Many other legislatures are set out in a semi-circular format, which originated in ancient Greece. This shape allows shades of opinion, literally from the left to the right, and tends to encourage the formation of party coalitions. Legislative buildings have always recognized that the public should be able to see and hear what is being done in its name, but it is only recently that it has become of great importance. Foster and Partners' Greater London Authority building and additions to the Reichstag in Berlin both have glazed public galleries overlooking the legislative chambers.

The architect A W N Pugin, who designed the ornament in the Palace of Westminster, remarked of the building: 'all Grecian, Sir; Tudor details on a classic body'. The symmetrical, axial plan was indeed an example of a type of layout that had been developing since the Italian Renaissance in the sixteenth century. The Renaissance interest in the meaning of fundamental geometrical forms meant that, for the first time since the ancient Greeks and Romans, it became possible to think of most buildings in abstract terms as formal symmetrical compositions – rather than as additive structures entirely driven by practicalities. This could cause problems. Renaissance artists and architects, including Michelangelo, Leonardo and Donato Bramante (*see plate 2.36*), were fascinated by the idea of the circular church. But when Michelangelo's great centralized design for St Peter's in Rome was enlarged after his death, it was given a long basilican nave better suited to its practical function. Similar problems could occur in the palatial public buildings of the nineteenth century designed according to the teachings of the Ecole des Beaux-Arts in Paris. When the majestic central spaces of the new Victoria and Albert Museum opened in 1909 they were found to be too large and high for the effective display of much of the collection. But these were exceptions. In fact, much of the story of public architecture from the Renaissance to the end of the nineteenth century is one of a careful combining of the symmetrical ideal plan with practical needs. The models were usually antique and appropriate to function. Temple plans were useful for churches. The oval amphitheatre was adapted for auditoria and lecture theatres. The sixteenth-century architect Andrea Palladio used the dimensions of Vitruvius's Egyptian Hall for large public rooms. Especially important as examples for civic buildings were the Roman baths, with their sequences of great public rooms of different sizes and shapes and the layout of such schemes as Hadrian's Villa near Rome, with its pools and curved colonnades.

These examples were particularly inspiring to the architects working from the middle of the eighteenth century onwards, who visited Rome as part of their architectural education. It was a period when Enlightenment ideas of social utility held sway. For the first time the idea emerged that by going back to basic principles, usefully and appropriately designed buildings could improve the quality of life. At the same time the growth of new social, public and political institutions and the demands of a modern economy created a need for a huge range of new types of building. It was an exciting moment for architecture. In addition to the usual palaces and churches, the academic exercises of French architectural students of the 1760s to 1780s included theatres, hospitals, markets, schools, libraries, fountains, baths and amphitheatres. By 1850 almost all the types of public and commercial building known today had been invented, including prisons, museums, offices, department stores and railway stations. The twentieth century, by contrast, added relatively few to the list, the most significant being the multi-storey car park, the airport and the out-of-town shopping mall.

Most of the public and commercial buildings of the nineteenth century were designed from a new rational standpoint that is now general: the architect has to think about the technical problems of building materials and most efficient organization of space as well as style and exterior form.

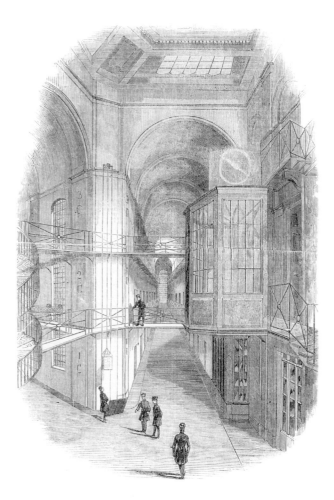

1.41 Interior of the Modern Prison, at Pentonville, London. Illustration from *The Illustrated London News*, 7 January 1843.

The prison, designed by Joshua Jebb, was built 1840–2. It housed 520 prisoners on the 'separate' system: one prisoner to a cell, each engaged in useful labour. V&A: NAL PP10.

Being efficient

Efficient planning had of course long been part of the design of places of manufacture and storage. The ropewalk at the Arsenal in Venice, erected 1570–90, is a single enclosed space 380 metres long. Positioned near the covered building slips and the stores of wood and canvas, it is part of a veritable production line for the rapid making and provisioning of ships. Later developments were crucially linked to innovations in materials. The introduction, at the end of the 1700s, of textile machinery created a demand for multi-storey mills with large clear floors. The floors were at first supported by wooden frames, which were later replaced in cast iron. Reinforced concrete expanded things even further: the multi-storey Fiat car factory at Turin, built in reinforced concrete between 1915 and 1921, covers 40 hectares. On its roof is a test track for the finished cars. Concrete also made possible the enormous storage silos and multi-storey factories of the USA in the early twentieth century.

Efficient planning has also had an enormous impact on the design of buildings for large numbers of people. One of the most striking and earliest examples was the Panopticon penitentiary invented by the philosopher Jeremy Bentham at the end of the eighteenth century. His aim was to replace the terrible prisons then existing, and thus stop transportation to the colonies. The scheme proposed a large glazed circular building with cells around the outside, in which prisoners were to be kept in solitary confinement under constant observation by a minimum number of warders. In its developed form, the Panopticon aimed to reform prisoners by seclusion, employment and religious instruction. The different classes of prisoners were kept in radiating cell blocks which could be observed from a central point. The reforming effects of isolation were often carried into prison chapels, by dividing them up with radiating screens so that each prisoner could only see the priest.

At school

The Panopticon principle was also applied on occasion to schools. This was not surprising, for the design of schools over the last 200 years has been a very accurate barometer of changing views on the purposes of education. Advanced British schools of the 1830s introduced standards of design and space for children. They were places of production, in the words of a contemporary commentator, of 'the division of labour applied to intellectual purposes; the principles in schools and manufacturing are the same'. A room that would now hold 30 pupils held 60, but the teaching methods were not those of today. Different groups of children were taught in the same room by child monitors, under the supervision of the head teacher. Raised benches helped the children to see the monitor. A concern for proper ventilation meant that ceilings were 3 to 4 metres from the floor, but windows were placed high up to prevent distractions. They also gave the best light for writing. Even with a rule of silence, the noise must have been terrible. Following the Education Act of 1870, which was prompted by the need for an educated workforce, classes went into separate rooms and were seated in rows of desks facing the blackboard. Large windows on the left meant work was not shadowed, at any rate for the right-handed. Ceiling heights rose to 4.26 metres. Boys and girls had separate entrances, on different streets if possible, and separate playgrounds. After 1900, concerns for cross-ventilation and for more light led to the pavilion system, in which classrooms were built not around a communal hall as before but in projecting wings. Gradually, beginning with infant and nursery schools, the idea took hold that the whole environment of a school could contribute to a child's education. Distinctions were made between noisy and quiet, and clean and dirty spaces. In the 1930s windows were made larger, sometimes covering the whole sunny south side of the school in the belief that low light levels damaged the eyes, although the results were often glare and over-heating.

In Britain, 11,000 new schools were built between 1945 and 1970 for an Education Act that gave free secondary schooling to all. It was an immense experiment in social idealism, reflected in buildings designed by architects who had not only imbibed the ideas of the Modern Movement, but had also studied the ways in which people actually behave in buildings. Unlike most previous school building, which had often spent as much or more on the exterior embellishments as on the interior, the new schools were truly designed from the inside out. The rigid hierarchical plans of the past were replaced by schemes in which distinctions were blurred between communal spaces and classrooms. Flexibility and informality were the key, matching contemporary educational theory. As school populations grew and economies of scale became more important new forms of planning were needed for very large schools – some of which utilized aspects of commercial and office design, including street-like corridors, atria and space planning reflecting the contemporary open-plan office.

1.42 Design for an expanding nursery school, 1934. Ernö Goldfinger.

The design was commissioned by the Nursery Schools Association in England, to expand school provision by providing cheap standardized buildings that would provide plenty of light and air. Pencil and coloured crayon on tracing paper. RIBA Library Drawings Collection.

1.43 Interior, Johnson Wax
Administration Building,
Racine, Wisconsin, USA, built
1936–9. Frank Lloyd Wright.

At the office

The office building, now so dominant, is a surprisingly recent arrival. It was only in the middle of the nineteenth century that processing the paperwork of business concerns and the government civil service became onerous enough to need specialized buildings. The development of office design has always been closely tied to business practice, management theory and mechanization, as well as to building technology. The first offices were suites of small separate rooms. As office buildings grew, the problem was getting enough light and air to masses of rooms and their connecting corridors. One answer was to use light-wells, modelled on the courtyards of the Renaissance *palazzi*. A scheme for British government offices of the 1860s proposed a continuous glazed light-well and galleries, very like the top-lit system used in Panopticon prisons. From the outside such buildings often look impressively bulky, giving no hint of the system of light-wells and courtyards within. The mid-Victorian office clerk had a high status. Everything changed with the coming of the mass-produced typewriter in the 1870s, and later the telephone – and with the ideas of the American Frederick Taylor, who analyzed the organization of work as a series of repeatable steps. Efficient office design closely reflected a firm's organization, showing the lines of authority, the separation of functions and the direction of work through different departments. Workrooms for clerks were to be as large as possible. Frank Lloyd Wright's Larkin building of 1904, for the mail-order department of a soap company, was a single space built around a huge top-lit central atrium. Occupying a noisy and restricted site it had no other windows, but boasted air-conditioning. It could accommodate 1,800 clerks and other workers processing 5,000 letters a day, many seated in fixed chairs. A later office building by Wright, the headquarters of the Johnson Wax Company of 1936–9, had a single, brightly top-lit and air-conditioned workroom of 2,281 square metres with a galleried mezzanine floor. Wright had a social design agenda for the whole office complex – it included a cinema for lectures and lunchtime entertainment. Herbert F Johnson aimed to bring 'employer and worker together ... When people get proper wages and proper working conditions they don't feel they need to organize to fight to get what they want'.

In side-lit high-rise office buildings, rooms could not be made bigger until the problems of lighting and ventilation had been tackled. Each floor of the concrete-framed office building of the Bata shoe company in Zlín in the Czech Republic, built in 1938, consisted of a large uninterrupted space. One of the lifts was in fact a fully-equipped air-conditioned office for the director Tomas Bata, able to open on and survey every floor. The Bata offices were lit on two sides and had natural cross-ventilation. Classic modern office buildings, like Mies van der Rohe's Seagram Building of 1958 (*see plate 4.16*), with its central core for lifts and services, have large numbers of small offices easy to air-condition. The advent of the modern large open-plan office reflected both new ideas in management and the availability of better air-conditioning. Its ultimate development, the so-called Bürolandschaft (or office landscaping) which emerged in Germany in about 1960, consisted of very large spaces informally arranged into status-free areas separated by plants and arranged according to individual choice. Most of the occupants were inevitably dependent on permanent artificial lighting, but views to day-lit windows were carefully preserved. A massive Bürolandschaft-based scheme of the mid-1960s by Sir Leslie Martin, which would have involved the demolition of most of London's historic government buildings in Whitehall, fortunately never came to fruition. In the 1970s corporate demands reintroduced desks in serried ranks: a Gas Board office in England was able to house 1,300 people in a single space. Since about 1980 office design has changed again. As we have seen, environmental concerns have reintroduced natural lighting and ventilation, frequently through a return to the atrium design pioneered by the Larkin Building. One of the earliest of the new atria, in Richard Rogers' Lloyds Building in the City of London, was partly determined by the organizational regulation that all the insurance brokers and underwriters should be in a single room and be able to hear the ringing of the historic Lutine Bell signalling good or bad news. Even more fundamental to changes in office design has been the computer revolution, which has not only made the ranks of typists disappear but also allowed people to work almost anywhere, including in their own homes. Large open-plan offices remain, but with desks (and smaller offices) used by many different people. Desk systems are carefully arranged to give appropriate privacy within the minimum area. In some places, like Scandinavia, there has been a return to small individual offices for all.

1.44 (above) Lloyds of London, London, 1978–86. Richard Rogers Partnership.

1.45 (opposite, above) Design for the railway station, Scarborough, Yorkshire, England, 1844 (built 1845). George Townsend Andrews.

Pen and ink and watercolour. V&A: 8936.14.

1.46 (opposite, below) Waterloo International Terminal, London, 1988–93. Nicholas Grimshaw & Partners.

The terminal takes cross-channel high-speed trains. RIBA Library Photographs Collection/Reid & Peck.

People on the move

Like offices, specialized transport buildings are a comparatively recent innovation. They all serve three basic needs: processing the passenger on arrival, waiting and a safe delivery to the bus, train, plane or ship. The basic parts were already present in the railway stations of the 1830s: ticket halls, waiting rooms, refreshment rooms, lavatories and covered platforms. From 1840, stations often also included a hotel. They have changed little in the last 150 years, except for the needs of the trains themselves. New stations do not need the tall sheds of the past, designed to take away steam and smoke. The canopy of the Channel Tunnel terminal at London's Waterloo is designed to flex as the immensely long train speeds into the curved station built on top of a viaduct.

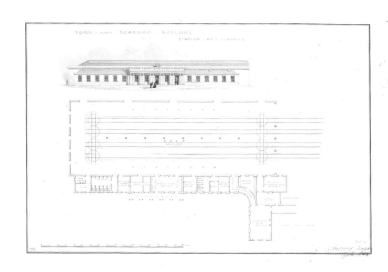

Shops and shopping

The design of shops is different from that of most other buildings. Shops exist to show goods and get people to buy them. The impressive external architecture of department stores like Selfridges in London, or its much newer branch in Birmingham, is designed only to attract us to the building by its distinctive design. Once we are inside, we are there only to look at the goods. On the face of it, going shopping is very different from the experience of being pushed through an airport. We are free to go where we want. Shopping is about individuality. What we buy (and where we buy it) plays an important part in how we see ourselves and the ways others see us. Shopping is about making and controlling our own world. In fact, however, shops, like airports, control you.

The challenge of shop design has always been to get the greatest number of people past the largest number of goods. Technical advances have played a large part in this process. Cast iron and glass helped to make possible the first covered shopping arcades at the end of the eighteenth century. Shop design was revolutionized by the advent of plate glass for street windows in the mid-nineteenth century. Lifts and escalators were key to the development of the large department store. The first purpose-built department stores, put up in Paris in the 1850s, were showplaces of technology and rational organization. The Samaritaine store in Paris had steam heating, electric awnings and a conveyor belt to carry goods from the shop floor to the delivery department. Samaritaine's central atrium, built about 1907, not only enabled the maximum number of goods to be seen, but also acted as an elegant space in which its bourgeois customers could see and be seen. The shop's role as a centre for a particular class only served to increase sales.

Department stores were, from the start, celebrated for the range of goods on sale. Whiteley's in London was known as 'The Universal Provider'. But shopping in these stores was still a relatively formalized process. The idea of relaxed free choice in shopping arrived with the supermarket, first established by Ralphs Grocery Company in Los Angeles, inaugurated in 1928. According to the historian Richard Longstreth, Ralphs 'created a new kind of space that was lofty, imposing, yet non-hierarchical and conducive to perambulation, allowing consumers to choose their own paths of movement as well as their own goods'. In fact designers of supermarkets are able to influence our purchases – especially impulse buying – with lighting and presentation, and by the positioning of different goods.

Shopping malls combine the all-enveloping experience of the department store with the ideas of the supermarket. The form was invented in the USA in the 1950s by the émigré architect Victor Gruen, apparently inspired by the streets of his native Vienna. Shopping malls replicate the experience of the shopping street but place it under cover and under complete control. Seen from the car parks that surround it, the building is often a blank box. The streets are commonly laid out as a triangle, with a large department store as an anchor at each angle. All the other shops lining the streets have narrow frontages of identical size. The immense Bluewater, near London, seeks to attract eight distinct 'lifestyle groups', from 'young survivors' to 'club executives' (*see plate 4.32*). Its three streets each have a distinctly different character, reflected in their decor and lighting as well as the type of shop: one a traditional high street, aimed at families and children; another elegant and classic, selling fashion labels; and a third media-based and youth-oriented. Bluewater aims to be a complete experience, with a leisure village attached to each street as well as outdoor activities. Shopping malls are filled with directional signs but the centre's real purpose is to achieve the 'Gruen transfer'. This is when we get distracted from what we came to buy and start to wander, eventually getting lost in a disorientating world of processed air, piped music and eternal daylight. Only by going into a shop can we know why we have come and what we are meant to do.

1.49 La Samaritaine department store, Paris, about 1907. Frantz Jourdain.

structures of metal or reinforced concrete at the end of the nineteenth century opened up even greater possibilities. Thus London's Ritz Hotel of 1903–6 is constructed around a hidden steel frame. What we actually see are massive granite façades, more weightily designed at the bottom than at the top, convincing us that the building is a solid and stable masonry structure. The message of dependable solidity is clear. At the end of the twentieth century the same type of frame, but made of concrete, forms the structure of the high-tech Willis Faber Dumas building. Its curving glass curtain-wall panels float weightlessly, by day reflecting the surrounding buildings, by night revealing its interior and frame. Either way, it is a building trying to be invisible. From about 1850 to 1970 concerns about

2.3 Ritz Hotel, London, 1903–6. Charles Mewès and Arthur Davis.

visible and invisible structure were at the heart of critical debates about architecture in the West. Buildings with visible and comprehensible structures were thought to be more 'honest' and therefore more moral than those with concealed structures and sham finishes. The morality of a building reflected the morality of its occupants. Thus the buildings of the Arts and Crafts movement at the end of the nineteenth century adopted traditional visible construction methods, using bricks and timber, combined with methods derived from medieval handicraft traditions. Since the 1960s, critics and theoreticians have increasingly recognized that concepts of morality in architecture have no fundamental basis in design and are largely culturally driven.

2.4 Willis Faber Dumas office, Ipswich, Suffolk, England, 1971–5. Foster Associates.

The building is heated by natural gas and has a turf-insulated roof. RIBA Library Photographs Collection/Alastair Hunter.

2.5 Crown Hall, Illinois Institute of Technology, Chicago, USA, 1950–6. Ludwig Mies van der Rohe.

RIBA Library Photographs Collection/Marius Reynolds.

2.6 *The Mad King's Castle* (detail), about 1900. Percival Gaskell.

Schloss Neuschwanstein was built 1869–80 for King Ludwig of Bavaria. Etching and mezzotint. V&A: E 39–1913.

Basic design

Creators of buildings have for centuries used a number of tried and tested design approaches that are known to create predictable reactions in the viewer. The most universal of these use alignment, scale, proportion, interval and site. Long, relatively low horizontal structures, for instance, tend to invoke ideas of calm, dignity and reassurance, all the more so if their outline is clean and uncluttered. The message is further reinforced if the building's plan is symmetrical, and its façade divided up vertically into regular units. This idea can of course be seen in the classical buildings of ancient Greece, but the same approach is also visible in much more recent architecture, especially that of the second half of the twentieth century. Tall, relatively narrow vertical structures, on the other hand, tend to give out messages of excitement, especially if their outlines are complex and irregular. The message is further reinforced if the ground plan is not symmetrical. This is the case in many medieval buildings, which were designed in the additive manner as a group, so that structures of different height and shape reflect different functions. It is therefore no accident that the most obvious examples of this approach to design are romantic imitations of medieval castles in dramatic natural settings, or their close cousins, the spiky wooden nineteenth-century houses of North America,

which have become a cliché of horror films. A third design approach has only fully emerged since the complete development of computer-aided design in the 1990s. Labelled 'complexity architecture' by the critic Charles Jencks, it covers buildings with very different messages, including Libeskind's Jewish Museum in Berlin, and Gehry's Guggenheim Museum at Bilbao (*see plates Intro.11 and Intro.12*). What they have in common is a free approach to design, related to landscape and the natural world or to mathematical concepts (also found in nature) such as fractals. The result is often a total rejection of the old distinctions between walls and roofs, and a dramatic sense of arrested movement. We are reminded of the philosopher Schopenhauer's description of architecture as 'frozen music' and it is certainly true that the vigorous forms of Libeskind's buildings, and those of architects like Zaha Hadid and Coop Himmelblau, in fact share some of the same formal effects as the buildings just mentioned.

Scale and proportion

Scale and its cousin, proportion, are among the most important weapons in the design armoury of the architect. Visual scale is about one thing in relation to another. It is all a matter of visual impression. By clever use of scale, bulky buildings can be made to look friendly and welcoming. Conversely, small buildings can be made to look monumental. Our impression of scale is crucially related to our natural tendency to look for visual clues of size. A façade made of a few stone blocks (which we assume to be large) is more imposing than one made of thousands of bricks (which we assume to be small). Above all, we look for things that we imagine relate to our own size. In designing skyscrapers, architects usually ensure that what we can see at street level is at a human scale. In older skyscrapers the lower parts often take the form of a visually separate, relatively low building – while at the top is another visually distinct construction.

2.7 *Wall Street*, 1915. Paul Strand.

We often assume that elements like columns or window openings relate comfortably to our own size. In this photograph the intimidating scale of New York is shown by how tiny people look against the column-like elements between the dark openings. Platinum print, made 1990. V&A: E 2498–1992.

BUILDINGS WITH MEANING:
HOUSES OF PARLIAMENT, CAPITOL, REICHSTAG

Michael Snodin

The buildings we create to house our legislatures carry a huge weight of meaning. In democracies, including those that are monarchies, the parliament is usually the leading architectural symbol of the nation. Its design has to express how the nation sees itself, and wants to be seen. The legislatures in Washington DC, London and Berlin, therefore, show very different design approaches.

The Capitol in Washington has been a national symbol since the very earliest days of the United States. It was built to house the Library of Congress and Supreme Court as well the Senate and House of Representatives. To George Washington and Thomas Jefferson, the Capitol was the most important building in the new federal capital planned in 1791, placed on a hill as the focus of the radiating avenues of the new city. Writing to the city's designer, Pierre Charles L'Enfant, Jefferson hoped that the Capitol would be based on 'some of the models of antiquity which have the approbation of thousands of years'. The building we see today was begun in 1795, partially destroyed by British troops in 1814 and only completed, in an enlarged form, in 1916. But throughout this long period the basic design did not change: a building in the classical style with a prominent dome and triangular-pedimented portico supported by columns. The style of ancient Greece and Rome, with its messages of democracy and opposition to tyranny, was filled with meaning for the young republic. The symbolic decoration of the building accurately reflects changing ideas of American nationhood. Inside are columns of 1803 in the American Order, based on corn-cobs and stalks. Outside, sculptural groups celebrate *The Genius of America* (1825), the *Progress of Civilization* (1850) and the *Apotheosis of Democracy* (1916).

The Houses of Parliament in London, the largest secular Gothic building in the world, was begun in 1836 and finished in the 1860s. Officially called the Palace of Westminster, it occupies the site of a royal palace founded in the eleventh century. A fire in 1834 almost completely destroyed the medieval palace, which had ceased to be a royal residence three centuries earlier. The rules of the architectural competition stipulated that the new building should be in either the Gothic or the sixteenth-century Elizabethan style. As with the Capitol, these styles expressed national ideals linked to the past. Both recalled periods in which Britain was being shaped as a nation, and democratic forms and systems were being set up, as well as acknowledging the medieval palace, some of which survived. The building is decorated inside and out in a late Gothic style matching part of Westminster Abbey close by. While Gothic has lost its meaning as a national style, the Palace continues to be a potent national symbol, exuding a sense of history. This is something to do with its distinctive silhouette beside the River Thames, with the 98-metre-high Victoria Tower at one end marking the state entrance, and the shorter Clock Tower at the other. The Clock Tower, isolated at the end of the enormous building, has become a symbol in itself. This is because the clock, called 'Big Ben' after one of its bells, has become the nation's timekeeper, mainly thanks to the medium of news broadcasting.

The Reichstag building in Berlin is a living symbol of Germany's turbulent history. It was opened in 1894 as one the key official buildings in the capital of the new German Empire, housing the Federal Council (Bundesrat) and the Imperial Diet or Parliament (Reichstag). Partly burnt down in 1933 – in a fire widely suspected to be the work of the Nazis themselves – and heavily damaged during the Second World War, it languished until 1960 as a near-ruin. But its symbolic significance remained. In 1991 the building was chosen as the future home of the Bundestag (Federal Parliament) of the reunified Germany.

The Reichstag's confused combination of elements of baroque and Renaissance styles reflected late nineteenth-century uncertainties about what exactly a German national style should be, and by the 1890s domes and pedimented porticoes had become clichés of official architecture. But this dome was remarkably radical, a glass-and-steel structure that symbolized modern democracy. The 1990s reconstruction, which replaced the gutted interior with high-tech steel and glass, was not originally intended by the architect to have a dome. In the end the wishes of the parliamentarians won, but the glass dome has become a new kind of symbol. By day it allows the public to see the Bundestag at work and reflects light into the chamber. By night its illuminated form signals the continuing presence of the democratic process.

2.11 (far left) The Capitol, Washington DC, 1793–1916. William Thornton, Benjamin Henry Latrobe, Charles Bulfinch, Thomas U Walter, Montgomery C Meigs.

2.12 (left) 'Big Ben' on New Year's Night, Palace of Westminster, London.

2.13 (right) The Reichstag, Berlin, in about 1900. Paul Wallot. It was built 1884–94.

2.14 (below) The dome of the Reichstag, Berlin, as reconstructed 1992–9. Foster and Partners.

2.15 Houses by the O'Rosin (now O'Donovan Rossa) Bridge, Dublin, 1790s.

RIBA Library Photographs Collection/Edwin Smith.

according to those of an Order which is not actually present (*plate 2.15*). The classical Orders, like the modular systems just described, were also a scaling device – for the Greeks and Romans saw each Order as a person, with a head-like capital and body-like shaft. Their proportions and decorative forms reflected certain human types: the squat and heavy Doric, a well-built man; the slimmer Ionic, a graceful girl. Thus a proportional system was transformed into a device that was able to give buildings very specific meanings – the Doric Order was used for temples dedicated to the manly gods; the Ionic for goddesses and for the god of the arts, Apollo.

Signs and symbols

The meanings of Greek temples are but one example of architectural messages that spring from particular cultures. Today we are surrounded by such specific architectural signs, in particular those that tell us what a building is for – a spire indicates a church, a sheer glass wall suggests an office, a *torii* gateway in Japan a temple. Such signs play an important part in making us feel at home in our built surroundings. But that is not to say that the same signs cannot say different things to different people or at different times. In the Islamic cultures from Turkey to South Asia, a dome (over the prayer hall) and one or more minarets (for the call to prayer) are the visual signals of a mosque. In early twentieth-century Dresden, however, the same forms were borrowed to symbolize the exotic links of the Yenidze cigarette factory. As quotations, so to speak, from Islamic building they evoked quite specific associations and made a powerful and lasting impression on consumers of the product. Our reactions to such shifting signals are currently being tested by the adaptation of many buildings in the West to other functions. Some such changes work and others don't, depending on the power of association. Banks, with their solid and impressive design and often classical treatment designed to inspire customers' confidence, have turned into restaurants, while churches have been converted into apartments. While the first bank to turn into a restaurant was perhaps a little surprising, the formal grandeur of a banking hall now seems entirely appropriate to dining, while banks themselves strive to make their premises ever more informal and welcoming. A spire on a residential block continues to confuse us however.

Association and quotation

One of the most frequent forms of quotation in Western architecture is the portico, a classical motif of a triangular pediment above a pair or group of columns, one of the fundamental design ideas of Western architecture. The device was originally used on ancient Greek temples. Today we are very much aware of the extremely subtle ways in which Greek temple builders manipulated design and form. Systems of proportion and devices such as entasis, the manner of thickening a column to correct undesirable optical effects, gave their buildings a sense of clarity and repose which are key to our response to them. In looking at such Greek buildings we tend to link these design qualities to a notion of Greek culture as the birthplace of democracy and the cradle of European civilization. Inevitably, similar meanings have become attached to the pediment and column motif in more recent contexts. But it is useful here to remind ourselves that we are unsure what cultural or symbolic meanings the ancient Greeks themselves attached to the design devices of their architecture. Firstly, Greek buildings were not the white structures we see today, but brightly painted – at least in part. Secondly, their temples seem not to have been places of calm contemplation, but scenes of public animal sacrifice, their dark interiors closed to all but the priesthood. Some modern scholars have seen forms of symbolism in the design of the columns and their characteristic ornament that is far from calm and life enhancing.

But the expression of higher values is only one of the modern messages of ancient Greek forms, for the same forms were adopted and used in the buildings of ancient Rome. For centuries, reactions to ancient Roman buildings were conditioned by a particular cultural memory of what Rome stood for. Rome after its fall represented a lost ideal, a civilization whose values and culture were desired and whose empire was envied. The ruins of the lavishly decorated buildings in Rome itself, as the most evident remains of that civilization, had a special fascination, most notably for the architects of the Renaissance from the fifteenth century onwards. Since then, classical architectural elements (and the pediment and columns in particular) have become powerful signals of elevated status and power – on the palaces of rulers and on official and public buildings of all sorts from parliament houses to libraries, and even imported as a mark of distinction in the anonymity of modern housing developments.

The complexities of associational design are also strongly shown in the design of roofs. This might seem surprising, as the shapes of roofs are of course largely determined by climate. But it is precisely because of this that roofs have taken on cultural and symbolic meanings. In Britain, for instance, the currently popular designs for houses and even blocks of flats have markedly pitched roofs. This is part of a preference for generally backward-looking forms and details – in this case a revival of a late-nineteenth-century style, which had itself plundered earlier styles. Why should this be? At an immediate level, perhaps, is the appeal of obviously traditional forms at a time of rapid change. This was certainly one of the main reasons the style was popular a century ago. But why is the pitched roof now so often preferred even when divorced from other backward-looking elements? By using the right materials, the drawbacks of flat roofs in a wet climate have been overcome, so it must be something cultural. It is interesting to recall here the cultural and political meanings of pitched and flat roofs in the 1920s and '30s. The Nazis, linking traditional building forms with climatic and racial theory, promoted the pitched roof as the Aryan ideal for houses, and associated flat roofs both with the Middle East and with the International Modern style, which they linked with communism. For International Style architects, however, flat roofs were the symbol of a new rational universal architecture promoting social betterment. But improvements in the quality of life were also the aim of Arts and Crafts architects around 1900, whose pitched roofs and traditional treatments lie at the root of the modern house style (*plate 2.17*).

2.16 Youth hostel, Detmold, Germany, about 1934. G Prolb and W Euler.

RIBA Library Photographs Collection.

2.17 Design for Broadleys, Cartmel, Lancashire, England, 1898. Charles Francis Annesley Voysey.

Pencil and watercolour.
RIBA Library Drawings Collection.

Looking at style

The most usual way of approaching the study of architecture is to consider the changing styles or 'looks' of buildings. It is possible to think of the story of style in terms of broad formal movements or traditions, some touching and overlapping and others independent, emerging from practical, social, political and religious needs as well as available materials and technology. Style involves the whole approach to a building's design, including the relationship between a building's structure and its form, the handling of materials and the way it uses basic design devices, and the type of signs and symbols just discussed. Knowing this, the normal way in which we identify styles, mainly in terms of distinctive types of decoration, may seem rather simplistic. In fact this method continues to be the best route to begin answering the question that often faces us in looking at buildings: when was it built? But what drives style, and changes in style, is the search for a form of building that has meaning.

How styles happen

Like new ideas in other areas of design, styles in architecture often emerge as an obscure and long drawn-out gathering of ideas and appropriate forms. It is, however, sometimes possible to identify a precise moment. In twelfth-century Paris, Abbot Suger created the Gothic style in building his new royal church at Saint Denis by using rib-vaults and pointed arches. Typically for a new style, neither of these were new ideas. Suger's achievement was to realize that by combining them he could create a structure that used light to model its interior forms. A century later, after many daring experiments in the cathedrals of northern France, a Gothic way of building had emerged in which the idea of the solid wall was largely abolished. In the Middle Ages, styles were spread as much by the travelling of architect-masons as by the desire of the clerical clients to build in a manner that matched that of their neighbours and outdid rivals. In Europe, since the advent of printing in the fifteenth century, books and prints (and, since the nineteenth century, magazines and photographs) have played an extremely important role in spreading new ideas. In 1665 Sir Christopher Wren went to Paris, not only to meet the celebrated architect-sculptor Giovanni

Lorenzo Bernini, (who was in Paris trying to secure the commission to build the Louvre), but also to 'collect all France on paper' – all in preparation for the building of St Paul's Cathedral. The ideas of the pioneering architect Le Corbusier, central to the Modern Movement of the twentieth century, were spread very largely through his own magazines and books, often in translation.

Style and originality

In today's architecture originality in design has a high value. The critic Charles Jencks, writing in 2002, identified 21 distinct styles or approaches to design in buildings put up since the 1960s. This emphasis on the new is by no means usual in the history of architecture, which shows architectural styles changing at very different paces, dictated by the cultures that have produced them. In vernacular architecture, everyday buildings designed according to local tradition, conservatism is the norm. Such buildings often stand outside the great style movements. Style change is often prompted by the demands of competing states or religious movements and by economic activity – which partly explains the very rapid style changes in Europe over the last 500 years. On the other hand, conservatism has often been promoted by religions, such as Hinduism and Jainism in South Asia, and underwritten by codified rules – canons of architectural conventions, like the Hindu shāstras – although for much of its history the Hindu temple has also developed dramatically within its own idiom, with different patterns of development in the north and south of the Indian sub-continent.

Conservatism may also be promoted by the forces of the state, frequently through the use of rules. The elaborate regulations governing the making and forms of Chinese architecture were set down in 1103 in a master builder's manual written by Li Chieh, an assistant inspector in the Palace Department of Public Works. The rules controlled every detail of design, based on a modular system of proportions. They persisted until 1734, when a new module was adopted by the Palace Office of Works. Rules can also emerge from the pursuit of perfection. In Europe, from the early 1500s, a huge effort was put into working out the perfectly proportioned set of classical Orders, using ancient treatises and actual ancient remains. The results appeared on the printed page, culminating in Claude Perrault's standard set of Orders of 1683 (*see plate 2.10*).

Insides and outsides

A useful way to approach the history of style in buildings is to think of it in terms of their treatment of interiors and exteriors – and how it throws light on meaning. The earliest cultures to produce a complex permanent architecture were in the eastern Mediterranean, particularly in Mesopotamia between the rivers Tigris and Euphrates, which saw the building of the world's first cities from about 3000 BCE. Their great stepped pyramids or ziggurats were the world's first monumental buildings, that is if we do not count the first Egyptian pyramid, built in stone as his tomb by King Zoser in 2778 BCE. A ziggurat was a man-made mountain, linking the earth and sky, at the top of which the priest-king sacrificed to the god. The great mud-brick structure of the ziggurat, like the pyramid, was essentially solid: it had no effective interior. This is not to say that there were no buildings with interiors, but we do not know if the mud built courtyard houses that made up Egyptian and Mesopotamian cities had interiors created with an eye to the meaningful experience of space. The first significant interior spaces that survive are Egyptian temples of about 1,000 years later. At the temple of Amun-Ra at Luxor beside the Nile, almost the entire space of the hypostyle hall is filled with 134 closely set columns, lit only by high windows. Each column imitates a bundle of papyrus reeds, with capitals formed as open and closed papyrus flowers. The form of the columns not only reflects an origin in wooden construction but is also clearly appropriate to the fertility god Amun-Ra, to whose dark sanctuary the hall and colonnaded courtyards lead. The extreme conservatism of Egyptian building is well shown at this temple, which was begun in 1408 BCE but completed in the same style 1,000 years later.

South Asia

2.18 The Great Stupa, Sanchi, India, first century CE.

The architecture of Egypt and Mesopotamia came to an end at the beginning of the Christian era. The Buddhist, Hindu and Jain architecture of South Asia, which is still very much alive, first emerged as the great styles of Egypt and Mesopotamia were nearing their end. These buildings were far from isolated from developments in other areas. Just as the Indian religions grew from (and continued to preserve within themselves) elements of earlier beliefs, in Indian architecture of the Mauryan period (c. 323–185 BCE) can be seen forms and ideas at times absorbed from Persia and other parts of Asia – including some incorporated, in turn, from ancient Greece. Buddhist architecture of the Gandhara region on the north-western edge of the subcontinent, from around the second to fifth centuries CE, shows strong influences from the Greek and Roman world in the style of its sculptural reliefs. Of all the world's great religious architecture, Indian buildings, with their freight of complex symbolic meanings, are related to belief in every aspect of their design – ranging from position, to basic form, proportion and every detail of ornament. The Great Stupa at Sanchi, built in the first century BCE, encases a structure thought to date to the third century BCE. It may mark one of the burial places of the ashes of Buddha, who was born in the sixth century BCE. It is simultaneously a reliquary and a sacred site. Like all stupas, it is formed as an architectural diagram of the cosmos. The dome-shaped heaven encloses the world mountain. Like the ziggurat, the world mountain is stepped at different levels, rising from the level of mankind to that of the gods. The solid stupa is topped with a square railing and a finial of umbrellas, marking the axis of the universe and symbolizing the soul's journey to enlightenment. The mound is surrounded by a fence with four gateways facing the cardinal points of the compass, each marked with the symbols of the Buddha. The geometric forms of the fence and gates are reflections in stone of wooden fences from an earlier era.

Also connected to the idea of the world mountain are the forms of the Hindu temple. The small cave-like shrine-room which houses the image of the god is surmounted and marked by a piled-up structure rearing to heaven. In northern India they are called *shikharas*, or 'mountain peaks', which they do indeed resemble and symbolize. But they also symbolize a celestial palace. The buildings of the temple complex, including the gateways, carry a large amount of symbolic sculpture following a precise iconographical programme. The position, orientation, layout and proportions of Hindu temples are, in fact, based on a mathematical mandala (or formula for sacred building) related to the structure of the universe. The key to the mandala is the sculptural programme. While the small, confined space of the inner sanctum of the Hindu temple (and the dense sculptural programmes in some Indian sacred buildings) tend to militate against purely spatial effects in interiors, there are magnificent exceptions – notably in the open halls of the temples of the Jain sect and the south-Indian Hindu temples of the sixteenth and seventeenth centuries CE.

The clue to the cave-like interior of the Hindu temple sanctuary lies in the most extraordinary buildings of ancient India, the Buddhist shrines and Hindu temples cut from the living rock. With a strong message of symbolic values related to the mountain cave as a dwelling place of gods, the Buddhist halls and shrines accurately replicate in deep cut stone a type of wooden architecture now lost to us. Perhaps even more amazing are the Hindu temples cut out complete from the mountainside.

2.19 The Kailasa temple, Ellora, India, 757–75 CE.

RIBA Library Photographs Collection.

2.20 Lingaraja Temple, Bhubaneshwar, India, about 1020 CE.

2.21 The Palace of Earthly Tranquility, Beijing, built from 1406 to 1420. Rebuilt 1655 and 1675.

RIBA Library Photographs Collection/Bernard Cox.

2.22 Chinese bracket and beam roof system, 12th century.

a: capital block
b: lintel
c: column
d: bracket arm
e: block
f: cantilever

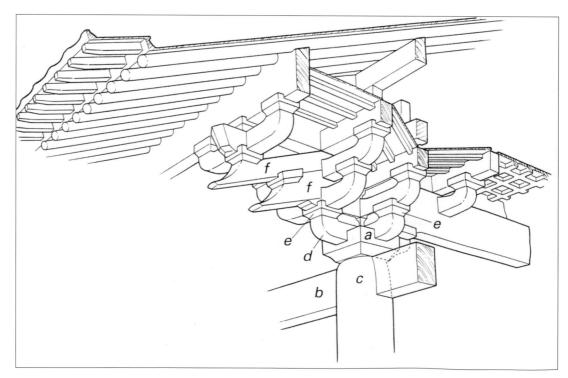

China and Japan

The traditional form of building in China, and the related architecture of Japan, was achieved by the first century CE and has hardly changed since. It is based on the use of wood in the trabeated or post-and-beam system, founded on a platform faced with stone or bricks. By filling in the spaces between the columns or leaving them open, buildings could be adapted to China's extreme range of climatic conditions, and the same basic design could serve almost any function, secular or religious. Security was obtained by surrounding groups of buildings with walls. The chief exception to the trabeated form was the pagoda – a borrowing from Buddhist India – often built of stone or brick as a shrine or reliquary, and imitating in its shape the umbrella symbol on top of the stupa and the mountain-forms of temples. The need to keep rain and snow off large open wooden structures, and to provide light as well as shade, has given Chinese buildings some of the world's most impressive roofs, with upswept lines and rich decoration. They are made possible by a roof-support system entirely unlike that of Western architecture, which is based on a truss, or triangle of timbers. In China, repeating and ever-shorter horizontal beams are held up by short vertical posts as the roof goes higher, allowing it to take on its characteristic curves. The great overhangs of the roofs are created by extending the column support with an elaborate system of clusters of interlocking brackets and sloping cantilever beams parallel to the roof. As Chinese architecture developed, many of these brackets and beams, picked out in bright colours, took on a purely decorative function.

In China's centralized government system, dominated by a ruling class of literate officials, architecture was always governed by laws, as we have seen with the builder's manual of Jie Li. Architecture provided a clear framework for the social system, the rank of a building's inhabitant being reflected in all aspects of its design, including the number of columns, the shape and complexity of roofs, the colour of roof tiles and the number and complexity of roof brackets.

But, as with the buildings we have seen in South Asia, Chinese architecture also reflected in its design a belief system based on an ordered and harmonious universe. All town plans and building plans symbolized the idea of the earth as a square in which each side corresponded to a cardinal point of the compass. Each point was associated with a set of colours, animal symbols and other elements. From the north, evil comes like the cold wind from Mongolia; while the south, that of the summer sun, is a good direction. In China buildings were, and still are, positioned by geomancers using feng shui (or 'wind and water') to favour the good spirits and repel the bad. Especially important is the positioning of openings. Buildings generally open to the south. In houses, a blank wall faces the visitor beyond the front door to deceive evil spirits. The fierce figures and animals which frequently crowd along the roof ridges are not mere decoration. Some serve to deter evil spirits falling from the sky, while others, like the dolphin finials, are symbols of water designed to avert fire. Belief systems also affect the positioning of activities inside the house: the good south and the west, linked to autumn and the white of mourning, made the south-west corner the place for honouring the ancestors.

Some of the most remarkable examples of the type of Chinese wooden architecture just described are in fact in Japan, where building began in that style with the coming of Buddhism in the fifth century CE. The Great Buddha Hall (Daibutsu-den) at Nara is the world's largest wooden structure. It houses an enormous statue of the Buddha, made in 749 CE. The increasing decorative elaboration over time of Chinese buildings was also seen in such Japanese structures as the mausoleum of the first shōgun at Nikko, every inch of which was covered with lacquer in a great display of power and permanence. The great hall at Nara, as often in Japan, repeats an earlier building – in this case an even larger structure, built in the twelfth century and itself a replacement of one built in the sixth century. At Nara the destruction was the result of fire and war, but replacement is often a deliberate act. The shrine at Ise, the most holy place of the pre-Buddhist Shinto religion, has been rebuilt in identical form every twenty years since its foundation in the seventh century. The careful attention to restrained form shown in the design of the Ise buildings is now

2.23 Katsura Imperial Villa, Kyoto, Japan, 1615–63.

2.24 Interior in the Katsura Imperial Villa, Kyoto, Japan, 1615–63.

regarded in the West as the leading characteristic of Japanese architecture, notably shown in domestic building. This was not always so: 100 years ago the West hugely admired the skilful and elaborate decoration of buildings like those at Nikko. In fact the Nikko mausolea were being built in the same period as the imperial villa at Katsura, one of the most famous examples of classic Japanese domestic building. These are single-storeyed buildings with large subtly shaped roofs carried on wooden columns as in China, but with the important difference that here the columns inside the building are arranged according to functional need, leading to an unbalanced arrangement. This same interest lies behind the planning of the whole building, a series of linked and interlocking pavilions asymmetrically disposed around a garden calculated to inspire poetry and contemplation.

The rooms are proportionally laid out to the *ken* module and *tatami* mat system, and are designed to be appreciated from a position sitting on the floor. The outer walls, which carry no weight, are made of plastered mud over bamboo, or are removable sliding panels in two layers – one in solid wood, the other in translucent paper. Within the rooms the sense of enclosure is maintained by a deep solid strip next to the ceiling. Internal walls are solid or sliding panels of opaque paper. The result is a building in which space is not modelled by light, as it usually is in the West, but in which the quality of light determines the materials and design. There is no sense that the building has been planned according to a predetermined scale of spatial experience, but rather, as Arthur Drexler put it: 'in the view which regards architecture as a kind of music, Japanese architecture is a thoughtful meandering along a keyboard'.

THE ART OF ARCHITECTURE   81

Ancient Greece and Rome

The architecture of ancient Greece has profoundly affected the way we look at buildings in the West. The Greeks adopted the columns and symbolic capital designs of Egypt and the eastern Mediterranean and gave them a new meaning dependent on the interaction of light and dark, space and mass. Greek temples are like immense sculptures in stone. This achievement was all the more remarkable given the limitations the Greeks imposed upon themselves. Although they knew how to build arches, they rejected their exciting possibilities, literally putting them down in the sewers. Greek builders concentrated most of their efforts on the exterior, notably in the form of the column-surrounded, or peripteral, temple. When their preferred post-and-beam system was translated from wood into stone in about 600 BCE its origins remained stubbornly evident in the Doric Order, with grooved triglyphs above the columns representing the exposed ends of the ceiling beams.

The central place of mathematics in the Greek world-picture, applied to the design of temples and other sacred buildings, transformed this limited vocabulary into one of the most subtle and versatile forms of architectural expression ever devised. The Doric temple of Hera at Paestum, of about 530 BCE, exudes a great sense of strength, its columns powerful and forbidding. A hundred years later the Athenians built the Parthenon, a victory tribute to the goddess Athena on the Acropolis and the greatest achievement of the high period of Greek architecture. It contains hardly a straight line. Careful curvature prevents the columns from appearing too thin and the base of the building from seeming to sag, while irregular spacing of the columns at the corners stops them looking weak. But this is much more than mere optical trickery, for it serves to turn the Parthenon into a building of immense harmony and grace, almost a living thing. These devices are combined with a use of sharply carved stone, and especially of marble, carrying out a fixed repertoire of shaped elements or mouldings that not only produced satisfying sequences of light and shade but also allowed rain water to run off efficiently.

2.25 (above, right) Temple of Hera, Paestum, Italy, about 530 BCE.

Paestum was the Greek colony of Posedonia. RIBA Library Photographs Collection/Edwin Smith.

2.26 (right) *Interior of the Pantheon, Rome*, about 1734. Giovanni Paolo Pannini.

The Pantheon was built 120–4 CE.

2.28 (opposite) The Colosseum, Rome, 72–82 CE.

RIBA Library Photographs Collection/Bernard Cox.

2.27 The Parthenon, Athens, 447–432 BCE. Iktinos and Kallikrates.

RIBA Library Photographs Collection/Edwin Smith.

But the Parthenon held a secret, for within the temple was the great statue of Athena contained in a hall surrounded by two levels of columns. If we exclude the amazing half-bowls of the Greek outdoor amphitheatres, this was one of the earliest large internal spaces to be treated for deliberate architectural effect. The architectural treatment of internal space was truly launched by the Romans, who conquered the Greek lands from the second century BCE. They took from the Greeks the Orders, and even added two new ones, the Tuscan (or Etruscan, a version of Doric) and the Composite, a combination of Ionic and Corinthian. But the Romans, although they used the Greek modular proportional system in the design of the Orders, in fact employed them in a completely different way. Except in certain temples, the Orders largely lost their structural function, being applied as decoration to solid walls or against arched openings. Roman buildings were an architecture of appearances, the adopted Greek elements acting as signals of civilization and authority. We have only to think of the triumphal arch, a Roman invention, built of arches, which were fully exploited for the first time, combined with the Greek Orders. Another example is the great amphitheatre of the Colosseum in Rome built in about 80 CE, in which the Doric, Ionic and Corinthian Orders are piled on top of one another, the heavier-looking Doric at the bottom, the lightest Corinthian at the top. But they are not only decoration, for they appear to be holding up the wall, giving us confidence in its strength and stability. In fact the interdependence of art, structure and use, described by the architect Vitruvius, is especially clearly shown in the architecture of the Romans with its wide range of specialized building types, conscious adoption of the Greek style and revolutionary use of concrete. Concrete made possible the seating for tens of thousands of spectators at the Colosseum, supported on a system of vaults and tunnels. Together with the use of arches, it also produced the huge interiors of the Roman baths, basilicas and other public buildings, as well as encouraging the creation of linked series of rooms of different shapes and effects, opening off each other in a changing drama of light and shade.

The most striking of all Roman interiors is that of the Pantheon in Rome (*plate 2.26*), built about forty years after the Colosseum as a temple to the whole group (or Pantheon) of the Roman gods and now the best preserved building to survive from ancient times. The exterior is dominated by a great portico with a double pediment, which largely hides the dome and rotunda behind it, making a clear link with Greek temples. But the closely spaced columns of the Parthenon have been replaced by a more spacious set, leading us into the shade of the portico and preparing us for the interior space lit only by the open oculus at the top of the enormous dome. The whole space can be seen as being in the service of religious ritual. Each of the pedimented niches (now dedicated to Christian saints) was dedicated to a deity and may have been aligned to match its position in the heavens. The space itself can be seen as a microcosm of the world, leading us from the earth levels of the floor and lower walls to the heavens represented by the dome. The central hole allows us to see through to the god Zeus's own dwelling place beyond the heavens and for Zeus to enter with his rain, thunder and lighting.

After Rome

The Roman interest in interior space reached its ultimate extension only after the collapse of empire in the West in the fifth century CE. It was the Christian Eastern Roman Empire of the sixth century under the Emperor Justinian that started an obsession with the interior in Western architecture that was to culminate in the Gothic buildings of the Middle Ages. Although centred on Byzantium (renamed Constantinople and now Istanbul) the Byzantine Empire stretched as far as Italy. In his churches, Justinian carried out an unprecedented series of experiments with interior space. Some are vertical and explore the effects of domes, others are horizontal and develop the idea of the Basilica, or colonnaded Roman public hall (*see plate 1.36*). While the interiors of the basilican churches continued the Roman tradition of clarity and mass, the domed buildings introduced a new approach: they were made to appear mysterious, weightless and immaterial. This was achieved mainly through the careful handling of light, the use of domes on triangular pendentives and the concealing of the supporting elements. This is very clear in the chief church of the Empire, the immense Hagia Sophia (or Church of the Holy Wisdom) in Istanbul, which is still one of the architectural wonders of the world. The design is a unique combination of a basilican plan with the domed forms of smaller churches. In one of the earliest surviving descriptions of the artistic effect of any building, Paul the Silentiary – in his opening sermon – said that the great cupola, 56 metres above the floor, seemed

2.29 Interior of Hagia Sophia, 1852. Louis Haghe after Gaspare Fossati.

Hagia Sophia was built 532–62 CE and later added to. It was designed by the geometricians Isidorus of Miletus and Anthemius of Tralles. In the 1840s it was restored by Gaspare and Giuseppe Fossati. Lithograph. V&A: NAL 63H4.

2.30 Hagia Sophia, Istanbul, Turkey, 532–62 CE with later additions.

not to 'rest on solid walls but to hang from heaven on a golden rope'. Much of this effect is created by the ring of windows at the dome's base, the chief source of illumination in an interior which seems to be filled with its own glowing light. The four huge piers holding up the great arches are hidden and the walls between them, pierced with arcades, seem weightless, creating a sense of volume without structure – in the words of Vincent Scully: 'a shell containing a dream'. The perfect proportions also add to the illusion, as commentator Procopius noted: 'Through the harmony of its measurements it is distinguished by its indescribable beauty.' The 'unstructural' effect is reinforced by the wall coverings of mosaic and panels of marble and the open-work capitals, in which the Roman Composite Order has been turned into an elegant flat pattern. It is only on the outside that we see the huge original buttresses and the other supporting structures added over the centuries, the final clue to this magic and an indication of the risks that the architects took.

2.32 (opposite) The prayer hall of the Great Mosque, Cordoba, Spain, about 785 CE.

RIBA Library Photographs Collection/Bernard Cox.

Islam

Hagia Sophia is now one of the great sights of a predominantly Muslim city. It was converted into a mosque in 1453, acquired minarets and inspired the great architect Sinan to build mosques across the Ottoman Empire based on its design. From the time of Muhammad's death at Mecca in 632 CE buildings adapted to Islam spread rapidly across the newly conquered territories. By 670 CE the Islamic armies had reached Kairouan in Tunisia, its ninth-century mosque now the site of the earliest surviving minaret. While the architecture of the Islamic lands from India to Spain was by no means unified in style, mosques shared certain features associated with their religious and secular functions that were both practical and symbolic, including the minaret and the prayer hall with, often, an arcaded court before it. Just as the form of the first Christian churches was adapted from basilicas, these features were sometimes first created by converting existing structures or using existing materials. The eighth-century colonnaded prayer hall at Cordoba, now the cathedral, is constructed from reused Roman columns roughly adapted. Also common to most Islamic architecture is a particular approach to exterior and interior. In one sense there is no distinction between insides and outsides. The great gates to mosque complexes, with their tall niches open to the weather, are both interiors and exteriors. The exterior of the Taj Mahal, a mausoleum, is as elaborately decorated as its interior. On the other hand, many Islamic buildings are turned inwards, reserving their most elaborate effects for rooms and courts whilst leaving the minarets and domes to make their maximum symbolic impact on the exterior. As at Hagia Sophia, interiors are a game of appearances. Walls are completely sheathed in a dazzling display of patterned and inscribed tiles or carved and painted plaster. Geometry is a leading element in much Islamic ornament, except that of East Asia. The architects, with their background in advanced mathematics and their use of brick and light materials like wood, were able to vault spaces and create domes that surpassed Hagia Sophia in their daring. But even then the effect of the vaults and other functional elements is enhanced by a dizzying array of entirely decorative ornament, notably the stalactite-like muqarnas (*see plate 3.18*). This approach is matched by ground plans which ignore major axes, adding elements in an informal manner as in the complex series of rooms and courts at the Palace of the Alhambra in Granada, built in the fourteenth century by the Muslim rulers of southern Spain.

2.31 The Suleimaniye Mosque, Istanbul, Turkey, 1551–8. Koca Sinan.

Medieval Europe

As Hagia Sophia was being built, Celtic monks in Ireland began constructing a tiny monastery on the top of Skellig Michael Island, 166 metres above the Atlantic. Its domed stone cells repeated a form of construction that had been in use since the Bronze Age. The achievements of Byzantine church building took centuries to reach a Europe overwhelmed by invasion following the fall of the Western Roman Empire. In the late eighth century Charlemagne, the new self-appointed emperor in the West, began his palace chapel at Aachen – based on the Church of San Vitale in Ravenna, built 250 years before. A little later, the Church of the Apostles in Constantinople inspired the form of St Mark's in Venice. Both the interior of St Mark's, glowing with hundreds of figures of saints and angels in mosaic, and the ingeniously made and daringly positioned structures at Skellig Michael, show the investment that the Church was putting into building – leading eventually to the most significant architecture of medieval Europe.

2.33 Bourges Cathedral, France 1190–1275.

Every aspect of a medieval church was dedicated to reinforcing the faith of the worshipper through ritual – set out as a journey from the exterior west front, up the high nave to the taller lighter presbytery in the east: the visible reserve of priests and place of sacrifice. The church's layout, structure, lighting, and painted and sculptural decoration all played their part. Interestingly, when major churches came to be built in large numbers across Europe after 1000 CE they owed little to the Byzantine example, but went back to the Roman ideas of the semicircular arch, column, capital and rounded barrel vault. Also revived was the Roman notion of a massive but concealed structure, albeit made of stone rather than concrete. Although the fairground-like colouring which once adorned the strong simple ornament of these Romanesque interiors did something to lighten their effect, they must always have relied on massive sculptural modelling for their impact. The small windows let in relatively little light, but this was not for want of trying to do better. The problem sprang from the heavy construction methods chosen. This is made clear by the greater number of windows towards the all-important east, but most significantly by the steady changes aimed at lightening the sculptural effect and reducing and refining the building's supporting structure. The solution lay in tackling the limitations introduced by semicircular arches and vaults. Semicircular tunnel vaults could cover a space of any proportion. However, much more interesting effects could be achieved by making two tunnel vaults cross at right angles, creating a groin vault. But semicircular groin vaults could only cover square spaces, hugely limiting the creation of useful building layouts. The first development came with setting the semicircular arches on small uprights (by 'stilting' them). This made it possible to cover a rectangular space. An even better way was to combine stilted arches with pointed arches, as happened in the side aisles at Durham Cathedral in about 1100 CE, where the weight of pointed arches is carried on tall half-columns rising from the floor (*see plate 2.2*). Durham also has some of the earliest rib vaults in Western Europe (they originated in the Near East). These involved much more than simply adding projecting ribs to the vault for the sake of appearances, for they turned vaulting from a heavy monolithic block into a frame structure in which the ribs carry the whole weight, allowing the panels in between to be relatively thin. The rib vault and the pointed arch rapidly turned the Romanesque style into its exact opposite, the Gothic style. The real breakthrough happened at St Denis, thirty years after Durham, where rib vaults appeared with four pointed arches. Within 25 years of St Denis the new style had spread to most of the great churches of northern France.

Gothic has been described as a style better suited to being built in iron than stone. It is certainly true that the brilliant daring of Gothic buildings was not matched in structural terms until the advent of cast iron in the nineteenth century. As with those structures, the building forces in the great Gothic churches are carried on a supporting skeleton in perfect equilibrium, rather than on solid walls. The new style's name, invented in the sixteenth century, linked it to the barbarian Goths who overran the Roman Empire. Gothic was the antithesis of the civilized notions of classicism with its trabeated Orders and rule-bound certainties. Gothic had no rules beyond the overriding need to create an interior experience that brought people closer to God through symbolism and sheer sensory impact. A series of audacious and dangerous experiments produced an architecture which completely dematerialized the interior, by reducing its structure, filling it with coloured glass and making it ever taller. Unlike ancient classical buildings, with their weight and emphasis on the horizontal, Gothic buildings appeared to grow unstoppably up from the ground. But there was a price to pay for this interior illusion. On the outside, the body of the building was surrounded by an open cage of buttresses. But unlike the builders of Hagia Sophia, the Gothic architect-masons made a virtue out of this structural necessity, continuing on the exterior the idea of lightness and transparency and turning the practical elements into decorative forms.

The details which we now see as indicative of the Gothic style, such as traceried windows and ornament derived from nature, all emerged from the structural beginnings of the style, but were nevertheless used in solid-walled buildings lacking in the stone acrobatics of the great churches. Many of these buildings were secular, such as the merchants' palaces along the Grand Canal in Venice – their Gothic windows and arcades slotted like a kit of parts into flat, stone-faced brick façades – or the great town and market halls of textile centres of the Low Countries (*see plates 4.2 and 4.13*). In northern Europe the Gothic fascination with open structures was especially shown in the wooden roofs of secular buildings and smaller churches, matching in their increasing complexity the rib systems of stone vaults. The most complicated English roof type, the double hammer-beam, in fact does more to suggest support than actually give it, many of the elements being entirely decorative (*see plate 3.5*).

2.34 Reims Cathedral, France, 1211–1481

The Renaissance

In the 1420s, while the double hammer-beam was being developed in England, the architect Filippo Brunelleschi built the Foundling Hospital in Florence. Nothing could have been further from the transcendental mysticism of the interiors of the Gothic cathedrals. In a sunny courtyard, cool semicircular arches rest on slim columns. Under the arcades, geometric vaults, uncluttered by ribs, seem to draw lines in space. All is clarity, balance and repose and our feet are firmly on the ground. This is not architecture seeking to take us out of ourselves, but one which reconnects us to the real world. The hospital was one of the earliest buildings of the Italian Renaissance, or rebirth, a term (coined in the 1870s) describing the return to classical forms and ideas in early fifteenth-century Italy. There was of course no sharp break from the Middle Ages; Brunelleschi's hospital emerged from an Italian building tradition which had never entirely thrown off Roman forms. But architecture expresses more clearly than any other form of Renaissance design the particular mix of Greek and Roman learning (particularly late Roman Neoplatonic philosophy) and Christian belief that lay behind Renaissance thought. Amongst its tenets was the idea that the physical world was fundamentally mathematical and that harmony and proportion, evident in both design and music, reflected the divine mind. The regular geometrical forms of the circle and the square, which had played a part in architectural design for centuries, were imbued with special meanings, the square representing the terrestrial world, and the circle the celestial. Man himself, as part of the physical world, was central and embodied the divine order. These theoretical ideas were combined with advances in understanding ancient buildings, spurred on by the close study of antique remains and the new appreciation – from about 1414 onwards – of Marcus Vitruvius Pollio's *De Architectura*, the only architectural treatise to survive from antiquity.

All this would now be of only scholarly interest had Renaissance architects not also been working to create for their own time an architecture based on antique precedent. Firstly they refined from the antique material a system of the Orders far more consistent than the Greeks and Romans ever had, giving the resulting set an almost magical significance. Secondly they strove to apply antique precedent to modern building types, modifying both as they went. The meanings of the individual Orders were Christianized: Ionic was thus suitable for churches dedicated to virgin saints, Doric to strong male saints. Both trends are visible in the Tempietto (or little Temple; it is only 13 metres high) in Rome, designed by Donato Bramante, the greatest architect of what is called the High Renaissance. The Tempietto marks the hole in the ground said to have been made by the cross on which St Peter was martyred. While all its elements are classical (except for the open balustrade), Bramante combined several different ideas into a new whole. It is,

2.35 (left) The Foundling Hospital, Florence, Italy, 1421. Filippo Brunelleschi.

RIBA Library Photographs Collection.

2.36 (right) The Tempietto, San Pietro in Montorio, Rome, 1502. Donato Bramante.

appropriately enough, built in the Doric Order and repeats in its round colonnaded form the sanctuaries of the Greeks and Romans. But Bramante has extended the round interior walls upwards to take a perfectly hemispherical dome (like that of the Pantheon). The whole building is composed of pure geometrical forms, giving it a nobility which belies its small size (9 metres across) and a sculptural solidity like that of ancient Greek temples. Its design exemplifies the definition of architectural beauty of the architect and theorist Leon Battista Alberti, who saw it as 'the harmony and concord of all the parts achieved in such a manner that nothing could be added, or taken away, or altered, except for the worse'.

Bramante's combination of dome and columns was often echoed over the next 400 years, from St Peter's in Rome to the Capitol in Washington DC. Although the plan of the Tempietto was perfectly adapted to its function, marking a place of martyrdom, centralized designs were for a while the ideal of an architecture that was more concerned with ideas, symmetry and harmony than purely emotional reactions to light and form. Finally, the Tempietto exemplifies the Renaissance idea of a building as a solid form in space. That this seems very obvious to us now is a tribute to the power of a Renaissance idea, which was derived in part from the invention (perhaps mainly by Brunelleschi) of single-point pictorial perspective. This way of looking at architecture was very evident in the two types of building introduced at this time that have had a huge influence on architecture up to the present: the villa and the palazzo.

The ancient Roman villa was a wealthy town dweller's country estate. When the idea was revived in fifteenth-century Italy, for a powerful new breed of wealthy bankers and merchants, the villas combined the forms and materials of traditional rural buildings with the classical language of architecture. The results were the first recognizably modern houses – with central, clearly marked entrances, and windows and other details ranged in a balanced manner across the façades. The idea of the villa as an isolated ideal building set in a landscape or garden was enormously influential. It led both to the great baroque-style palaces of the seventeenth century and the country house of eighteenth-century England, as well as many of the key works of Le Corbusier and other pioneering modernist architects of the twentieth century. This would not have happened without the example of one of the most influential and inventive of all Renaissance architects, Andrea Palladio. His villas around Venice played a series of variations on a central block and (often) added wings. Their exteriors and interiors were designed to harmonic proportions, but in other respects were extremely innovative; windows could be simply undecorated holes punched through the walls and for the first time pedimented temple-like porticoes appeared on fronts of houses. Palladio, like other Renaissance architects, took advantage of the technology of printing. His book on the ancient architecture of Rome became a standard work. Much more significant were his *Four Books of Architecture* (1570) that transmitted his ideas and designs down to the nineteenth century.

Palladio was also a leading architect of palazzo design, but not the first. The palazzo had developed in the fifteenth century from the fortress-like dwellings of the powerful magnates in Italian towns. Its sheer walls rose straight from the street and it often occupied a whole block of the city grid. Inside, very frequently, was an arcaded courtyard (*see plate 4.12*). The palazzo idea has been the essence of Western urban building ever since, its constrained site giving a unity to the whole street coupled with a freedom to build in almost any style. The first Florentine palazzi, which were built for bankers, topped off their walls with huge projecting classical cornices. These hid the roofs and finished the buildings off against the sky. Below the cornice architects were able to develop and expand the repertoire of the Orders and make them more flexible. These liberating developments included the giant Order, in which columns pass through several storeys, and the coupling of columns to allow more room for windows. Pairs of coupled columns first appeared on a house designed by Bramante for the Caprini family in about 1501. In the Palazzo Caprini the columns are raised on a 'rusticated' ground floor apparently made of rough stones. The status of the ground floor (containing shops) and the first floor (for grand living) are made very clear by these contrasting architectural treatments.

2.37 Villa Capra (or Rotonda), Vicenza, Italy, 1565–9. Andrea Palladio.

2.38 The House of Raphael (Palazzo Caprini), Rome, 1549. Antonio Lafrery.

The house was built about 1501, designed by Donato Bramante (demolished). Engraving. V&A: E 36767–1906.

Breaking the rules

2.39 The Scala Regia, The
Vatican, Rome, 1663–6.
Giovanni Lorenzo Bernini.

2.40 St John Nepomuk,
Munich, Germany, 1733–5.
Egid Quirin Asam.

The architectural forms of ancient Greece and Rome, as developed during the Renaissance, dominated
Western architecture until the middle of the nineteenth century. That is not to say that they did not
continue to change. In fact, the story of Western architectural style in this period is one of waves of rule-
breaking alternating with sharp returns to order. The rule breaking began early. The inventor of the giant
Order, the sculptor and painter Michelangelo, led it with his masterful grasp of the use of scale and space,
and of very personal forms loaded with feeling. In his palaces on the Roman Capitoline Hill the giant
columns alternate with shorter ones supporting the first floor. In his vestibule to the library of the
Monastery of San Lorenzo in Florence the whole room is deliberately unsettling, with its stretched scale and
columns and brackets which support nothing. Michelangelo started a trend that developed a hundred or so
years later into the baroque style, the exact antithesis of the calm and noble certainties of the Renaissance.
Interestingly, the two great masters of Italian baroque, Giovanni Lorenzo Bernini and Francesco Borromini,
were both sculptors before they were architects. Bernini's Scala Regia, the great staircase leading to the
papal apartments in the Vatican, shows very clearly the rhetorical nature of baroque. This is not architecture
happy simply to be itself, like the Tempietto. It emphatically exists only to say something, in this case about
the power of the Papacy. It is saying it by using theatrical illusion, not only in its tapering scenery-like
design, but also through its use of sculpture, paint and the dramatic handling of light.

   This art of illusion in the service of emotion exactly suited a propagandist age, in which Church and
State were struggling for supremacy across Europe. The post-Reformation efforts to bring people back to

the Roman Catholic Church produced an architecture full of vitality and loaded with vivid imagery conveying ideas of reassurance and salvation to the faithful. Nothing could have been further from the clarity and logic of the Renaissance churches. This is especially clearly seen in baroque ground plans, which were often oval with undulating pierced walls, while façades became a series of complex curves. The power of the Church within the Spanish and Portuguese Empires meant that some of the most extravagant and complex examples of the baroque church style are in India and South America, often combined with traditional local approaches to design. The baroque style also perfectly matched the political absolutism of the seventeenth and eighteenth centuries. Palaces built on a huge scale relied for their effect on the same combination of sculptural design and giant Orders that we have seen in the churches. On the east front of the Louvre in Paris, a huge colonnade is carried across a façade carefully modelled across its entire length. The message is one of control: of mastery of space, people and even nature. The palace of Versailles sits at the centre of a grand design of radiating streets in the town and radiating avenues in the gardens. The interiors of Versailles, with their endless galleries and enormous staircases, were calculated to intimidate and overwhelm. Even in parliamentary, Protestant England, baroque took hold – the twin domes of the Royal Palace at Greenwich dominating the Thames, and Sir Christopher Wren playing endless spatial games in the churches of the rebuilt City of London. In fact Wren's pupil, Nicholas Hawksmoor, was to design some of the most extraordinary baroque buildings of all, sinister essays in light and shade, their details borrowed from ancient Rome and Egypt.

2.41 San Carlo alle Quattro Fontane, Rome, 1638–77. Francesco Borromini.

2.42 East front of the Palace of the Louvre, Paris, 1667–70. Louis le Vau and Charles le Brun.

Back to the rules and breaking them again

The swing back to the rules of Greek and Roman (and Renaissance) architecture was already happening when Hawksmoor was designing his churches in the early 1700s. It was pioneered in England: largely due to the efforts of Richard Boyle, the third Earl of Burlington, a movement began to revive what Joseph Wharton, a commentator of 1753, called 'greatness' in architecture – in which 'every decoration arises from necessity and use, and every pillar has something to support'. In seeking a practical modern form of classicism Burlington turned to the architecture of Andrea Palladio and his seventeenth-century British follower, Inigo Jones. But the results were very different. This is made clear by comparing Palladio's Villa Capra with Lord Burlington's villa at Chiswick, in part derived from it. The Capra, in spite of its four porticoes, is relaxed and assured. Chiswick, by contrast, is nervous and a little over-elaborate, with its Corinthian instead of Ionic columns and complex staircases. It is in fact an assemblage of significant quotations of Palladian motifs, such as the dome from the Pantheon and the semicircular 'Diocletian' window derived from the Roman baths.

A second classical revival began in Rome in the 1740s. The motive this time was a reaction against the formal excesses of the late baroque style and more especially its more frivolous cousin, the rococo style. It originated

in paper designs by the students of the French Academy, and got its first theorist in the philosopher the Abbé Laugier. His *Essai sur l'architecture* of 1753 argued that the primitive hut, a wooden structure completely free of non-structural elements, should be the jumping-off point for all architecture. At the same time, the buried towns of Pompeii and Herculaneum were being discovered and the monuments of ancient Greece being measured and published for the first time. The result was an architecture that followed antique ideas much more correctly than ever before, but in a range of ways. In Britain Robert Adam combined his studies of antique and Renaissance ornament to create a new type of neo-classical decoration. In Paris, Jacques Soufflot took a more intellectual approach, creating from the Church of Ste Geneviève (now the Panthéon) one of the first buildings since antiquity to be substantially supported by its columns, including, remarkably, those around the dome. The ultimate development of this trend was the Greek Revival of the years around 1800, culminating in the Altes Museum in Berlin by Karl Friedrich Schinkel, with its astonishing unmodulated row of Ionic columns. But the theoretical basis of the neo-classical style did not stop there, for it led to architecture that was a visionary exercise in pure form with considerable emotional impact and meaning. It includes Étienne-Louis Boullée's famous scheme for a cenotaph to Sir Isaac Newton, a hollow sphere functioning as a planetarium. More practical exercises in pure form (using newly invented primitive 'Greek' elements) were the basis of the designs of Sir John Soane.

2.45 The Panthéon, Paris, 1755–92. Jacques Germain Soufflot.

2.46 (below) Design for a cenotaph to Isaac Newton, about 1785. Charles Etienne-Louis Boullée.

The 500-foot-high sphere is hollow and pierced with holes to act as planetarium by day. By night a fire was suspended inside to represent the sun. Pen and Ink and wash.

2.43 (above, left) The primitive hut, from Abbé Laugier, *Essai sur l'architecture*, 1753.

Engraving. RIBA Library Early Works Collection.

2.44 (below, left) Chiswick House, London, about 1725–9. Richard Boyle, 3rd Earl of Burlington.

RIBA Library Photographs Collection/Bernard Cox.

2.47 A view of the Wilderness, with the Alhambra, the Pagoda and the Mosque in Kew Gardens, engraving by Heath after Edward Rooker and William Marlow.

Sir William Chambers designed all three structures, built 1758–62. Hand-coloured engraving. V&A: 29428A.

New styles and new meanings

The emotional charge carried by the novel and sublime architecture of Soane and Boullée was part of a new way of looking at architectural meaning, associated with an exploration of styles that had begun in the middle of the eighteenth century and was to reach its culmination 150 years later. While changing architectural meaning had previously very largely been a question of modulating an established architectural vocabulary, it now became possible to choose from a range of styles which in themselves carried specific messages, and for buildings in different styles and with different meanings to coexist. An early sign were the buildings in the Royal Gardens at Kew near London, created in the 1750s. While a series of temples dedicated to the heroic themes of peace, war and classical gods were in the conventional classical style, the garden also included an Alhambra, a pagoda and a mosque – all carrying a thrill of the exotic – along with a 'Gothic cathedral' redolent of British history.

A hundred years later, faced with a rich indigestible menu of styles both historic and exotic, commentators worried that the nineteenth century had no unique style of its own. In England a 'battle of the styles' between the promoters of the classical and Gothic styles in public building highlighted the dilemma. The classical style was fast losing the moral weight it had carried since the Renaissance, but was still useful for its messages of financial probity or political power. The new moral style was the revived Gothic, with its revealed 'honest' structures and links to a Christian medieval society, which many saw as a way of solving the social problems and conflicts of the nineteenth century. Its disadvantage was its link to religious building. A real case for Gothic as the style of the nineteenth century was made by the French architect Eugène-Emmanuel Viollet-le-Duc, who saw the link between the use of cast iron and the skeletal structures of Gothic. Iron, the first new building material since the Romans, had made possible large fully-glazed structures, most especially the biggest of them all, the Crystal Palace of 1851 (*see Intro.3*). But these great engineering achievements presented problems in the context of traditional architecture, associated

2.48 The University Museum, Oxford, England, 1854–60. Benjamin Woodward and Thomas Deane.

as they were with temporary structures. At St Pancras Station Sir George Gilbert Scott's Gothic hotel and William Barlow's great train shed, although practically touching, simply ignore each other (*see plate 3.54*). In the end, the idea of iron Gothic failed to establish itself beyond such buildings as Deane and Woodward's University Museum at Oxford, built to follow the ideas of the reformer John Ruskin.

By the end of the nineteenth century a broad range of developments in Europe and the United States was breaking the stylistic logjam, as architects searched for forms of architectural expression that were both truly modern and also national. Common to all was a new synthetic approach, in which elements of earlier styles were combined into a fresh whole. A British combination of Renaissance and baroque elements in public buildings was significantly called the 'new free style'. In domestic architecture there was often a moral dimension, linked to bettering living conditions. In Britain the architects of the Arts and Crafts movement developed Gothic's moral message and many of its forms. They added to them ideas taken from pre-industrial vernacular and country building in a deliberate attempt to encompass the familiar and the ordinary. In Eastern Europe and Scandinavia similar design approaches were part of a revived nationalism. In the United States the most advanced ideas came from the hands of Louis Sullivan and his pupil Frank Lloyd Wright. The prairie houses of Wright had intense national meanings and conveyed them in a new language free of the associational messages of style revival, combining a brilliant handling of space with new forms of ornament. Similar developments were happening in Scotland with the work of Charles Rennie Mackintosh and in Austria. In Vienna, Otto Wagner's Imperial Austrian Savings Bank of 1904 combined a classically proportioned façade clad in marble panels with an interior answering his dictum: 'the greatest possible convenience and the greatest possible cleanliness'. In the banking hall, ventilation tubes made in aluminium (in 1904 a rare metal) rise from a floor glazed to let light into the basement. The exposed iron structure, partly clad in aluminium, is highly practical, like the pioneering iron structure of the Crystal Palace 50 years earlier, but – unlike the Palace – it is artistically treated.

2.49 The banking hall, the Imperial Austrian Savings Bank, Vienna, 1904. Otto Wagner.

RIBA Library Photographs Collection/Sherin Aminossehe.

2.50 The Robie House, Chicago, USA, 1908–9. Frank Lloyd Wright.

STYLE AND FRONT DOORS

Tanishka Kachru

The front door is a transition between the exterior and the interior of a building, and can reflect the character of both. It is a physical entry into the building and, at the same time, a microcosm of its architectural style: it can make a style statement. Along with other elements like windows, it is part of the architectural language that allows us to understand buildings.

The position and size of a front door are no less important than its materials and decoration. They provide clues to the status of the building and perhaps the tastes of its residents. In the house of the 1930s Hollywood movie star Dolores Del Rio, the architect Cedric Gibbons (also her husband) has tucked the front door into a corner – but draws attention to its importance with a deep Art-Deco style asymmetrical stepped surround that leads one towards it. The door itself, faced with an alloy of stainless steel and copper and a simple horizontal tubular handle, quite plainly announces the modernity of the house.

Most elements of front doors derive from function, rather than being purely decorative. Hoods were first placed over doors to throw off rainwater, and glass panels and fanlights added to illuminate dark hallways. The Doric doorcase at the Royal Crescent, Bath, fulfils all these functions while using the classical vocabulary of pediment, entablature and columns to dignify the entrance to the house.

The main entrance to the Glasgow School of Art, designed by Charles Rennie Mackintosh is an example of the door being used as part of a strong composition. The front door here is part of an ensemble that creates a focal point in the long front elevation of the building. The ensemble includes a two-storey oriel window, balcony, stair tower and a flight of S-curved steps leading up to the door. The subtle curve of the architrave around the main entrance rises into a central medallion featuring two kneeling women and a stylized

rose bush. These elements, and the use of decorative glass and metal panels on the doors, relate closely to the continental Art Nouveau style.

The symbolic and the decorative combine in the front door to a Chettiar merchant's house in Tamil Nadu, India. It is the threshold between the public and private space and has a ceremonial role that is conveyed through the symbolism of the ornamental carvings, depicting images of gods and goddesses showering wealth and prosperity on those entering through the doors. Made in the late nineteenth century, the intricate illupai wood carvings of the door – imitating the style used in South Indian temples – reflect the prosperity and piety of the merchants.

In the original front entrance to the Victoria and Albert Museum, style and symbolism are combined in the decorative bronze and terracotta relief panels. The Italian Renaissance style of the doors suits the iconographic programme devised by Godfrey Sykes in 1862–63. The Biblical inscription 'Better is it to get wisdom than gold' above the architrave, and the terracotta panels over the doors showing figures of 'Science' and 'Art', clearly proclaim the purpose of the institution. The relief door panels further reinforce this, each depicting a branch of the sciences or the arts, with figures of Bramante and Michelangelo representing Architecture and Sculpture respectively. The metal doors were originally gilded to make them more impressive.

A primarily symbolic style can be seen in Mexico at Chicanná, meaning 'Serpent-mouth House' in Mayan, built between 600 and 830 CE. A full-frontal monster mask, with teeth centred over the doorway, extends the width of the central section and probably represents Itzamna, the Creator-God. The fully open reptilian monster mouth with projecting teeth was guaranteed to inspire fear and awe in the minds of those entering through it.

2.51 (top, left) Front door of the Del Rio House, Santa Monica, USA, 1931. Cedric Gibbons.

2.52 (top, middle) Doorcase at Royal Crescent, Bath, England, 1767–75. John Wood the Younger.
RIBA Library Photographs Collection.

2.53 (top, right) Main entrance to the School of Art, Glasgow, Scotland, 1896. Charles Rennie Mackintosh.
RIBA Library Photographs Collection.

2.54 (bottom, left) Front door of a Chettiar merchant's house, Tamil Nadu, India, late 19th century.

2.55 (bottom, middle) Original front entrance doors to the Victoria and Albert Museum, London, 1868. James Gamble and Reuben Townroe (based on designs by Godfrey Sykes).

2.56 (bottom, right) Serpent-jaw doorway, Chicanná, Mexico, 600 to 830 CE.

Putting on the style

Although by the 1940s the modernist approach had come to dominate architectural thinking, by no means all twentieth-century buildings were in the modernist style. In Britain, for instance, private housing and public buildings continued to be built in traditional historical styles up to the 1950s. The 1920s saw the emergence of the glamorous and highly ornamental Art Deco style that merged in the 1930s with some of the superficial elements of modernism. In Scandinavia, classicism survived – stripped down to its essentials. It was one of the sources of a humanized variation on modernist architecture that had a great impact outside Scandinavia in the 1950s and '60s. Le Corbusier's work with raw concrete in the 1940s and '50s also had a great influence, notably on New Brutalist architecture in Britain in the 1960s and '70s.

The seeds of a reaction against the fundamental ideas of modernism were planted in 1966 by Robert Venturi's *Complexity and Contradiction in Architecture*. To Mies' dictum 'less is more', Venturi's riposte was 'less is a bore'. The gates were thrown open to a host of new approaches. Venturi's ideas fed directly into a postmodernism that rediscovered historical ornament, meaningfully used. Some postmodernist buildings added borrowed motifs to fundamentally modernist structures, others were a creative mix of quotations and ideas from many different areas, while a third group attempted simply to replicate the buildings of the past. As postmodernism emerged in the late 1970s, the modernist emphasis on technology was rediscovered in buildings that expressed their structures

2.60 Neue Staatsgalerie, Stuttgart, Germany, 1980–3. James Stirling and Michael Wilford.

2.61 Stockholm Public Library, Sweden, 1920–8. Erik Gunnar Asplund.

RIBA Library Photographs Collection.

2.62 Richmond Riverside, London, 1988. Quinlan Terry.

The scheme incorporates several historic buildings and imitates others, including Sir William Chambers' unbuilt Richmond Palace. RIBA Library Photographs Collection.

2.63 Jean-Marie Tjibaou Cultural Centre, Nouméa, New Caledonia, 1991–8. Renzo Piano Building Workshop.

The structures are made of glass, stainless steel and timber. RIBA Library Photographs Collection/Nathan Monger.

more openly than ever before (*see plate 3.1*). At the time of writing high-tech is the dominating style in corporate architecture the world over. The computer-aided design techniques that lie behind much of today's high-tech building have also made it possible to construct practically any shape or form. Architects like Daniel Libeskind and Frank Gehry explore form in a manner without precedent, sometimes based on mathematics or reflecting the world of plants and animals. At the other end of the spectrum two movements point in other directions, answering some of our most urgent current concerns. The first, sustainable architecture, can be high-tech, like the Swiss Re building, or made of straw bales (*see plates 1.3 and 1.4*), but it always seeks to answer the challenges of reducing the use of non-renewable energy. The second is concerned with counteracting the spread of Western styles across the globe. Communities are increasingly commissioning buildings that are frankly modern, but that respond to their cultures and backgrounds.

CHAPTER THREE
CREATING BUILDINGS
Eleanor Gawne

3.1 The Pompidou Centre, Paris, built 1971–7. Piano and Rogers.

Most of us live in houses built of bricks and mortar, and judging by the outside, we imagine that these hold the building up. Apart from those that we can see, we may be unaware of other materials or structures used because they are hidden from view. Sometimes we see the 'insides' of a building only when it is being demolished, or being constructed. During DIY, we might see elements of the structure. Usually we can't see the trusses that hold our roof up, unless we enter the attic space. The foundations are hidden in the ground. Even walls can be thicker and more complicated than we first think. They may be cavity walls, or covered up with tiles or plaster, so it is impossible to see what they are really made of. It is particularly difficult to determine how modern buildings are made, and how they stand up. Sometimes the materials may be unusual or innovative. They are often combined to make inventive structures, not instantly understandable.

Many buildings use cladding, which covers up the structure underneath. The building might have a wood or metal frame, with bricks used simply as a covering. What we can and what we cannot see in buildings can be confusing, especially if we think about glass-and-steel buildings, or concrete shell roofs. The structure might be hidden even if it seems explicit. Sometimes old structures are reintroduced, or adapted from other industries. Often financial considerations outweigh aesthetic considerations, in terms of deciding on materials and structure.

In the nineteenth century, 'truth to materials' and 'honest construction' were the subject of heated argument between some architects and writers who wanted to return to a more honest method of building, which they considered appropriate to a Christian country. Modern Movement buildings of the early twentieth century followed these principles. Increasingly, building structures have to be covered up for safety reasons, controlled by regulations. So some architects hang a 'pretend' structure on the exterior of the building, to signify what you cannot see. A classic example is Mies van der Rohe's Illinois Institute of Technology at Chicago (*see plate 2.5*). This is notable because I-beams (so called because the rolled joists are shaped in section like the letter I) are used as applied decoration on the exterior of the building. They are meant to look as if they are part of the frame, but here they are additional to the 'real' structure, exposed simply for aesthetic reasons.

The Pompidou Centre in Paris, on the other hand, is an example where the 'real' structure is exposed and emphasized so that it contributes powerfully to the aesthetic effect. Also, rather than hide away the building services – like electricity, water and air – as is usual, their pipes are painted bright colours and revealed on the outside of the building. They can be easily seen and, on a practical level, they are far more accessible for maintenance. In this case, the building's basic method of construction becomes part of its design or appearance; this kind of aesthetic has been termed 'high-tech' architecture.

From just these two examples, it is clear that basic structural principles often shape the way a building looks. But just by looking at the exterior of a building we cannot always deduce how it stands up, or what materials are used in its construction. A deeper understanding of construction principles and building materials can help.

Geology and local materials

Building materials, methods and technology have evolved considerably over time. Initially they were strongly conditioned by the environment. The very earliest buildings were created out of landscape, using local materials. In parts of prehistoric Western Europe, people used natural caves as their dwellings. Anthropologists call these people troglodytes. The Cones of Cappadocia in Turkey are a natural landscape of eroded tufa, where caverns have been carved within the rock by the local people over the last 2,000 years to make churches, granaries, stables and houses – the buildings being adapted as needs arise. Some materials are more permanent than others. Igloos, made up until half a century ago by the Inuit people of the Arctic region, were created using the only materials readily available to them, snow and ice. The nomadic culture of the Bedouin tribe in Egypt and the Sudan requires homes in the form of tents. These can be put up and taken down quickly in the desert, and are lightweight so that they can be carried as the tribe moves around according to where they find food for their animals. Today, many cultures still use 'found' materials for building, some of them quite surprising. In Nigeria, empty 50-gallon oil drums made of steel, the refuse of the oil industry, are flattened out and used to build dwellings. When grouped together such dwellings form shanty towns.

3.2 Cones of Cappadocia, Turkey, 1st century CE.

3.3 Little Moreton Hall,
Cheshire, England, 1559.

RIBA Library Photographs
Collection/Roy Herman
Kantorowich.

Vernacular structures

Vernacular styles of building, indigenous to a particular area or country, exist everywhere. They use certain constructional methods and materials according to the traditions of the region and local geology. In many places, you can tell where you are simply by looking at which building materials are used. For instance, in Egypt and parts of Central America vernacular buildings use adobe or earth structures, the walls dependent for stability on their mass.

In Britain, stone and brick walls or timber framing are the main vernacular types. Often the structure is exposed on these types of buildings. In Britain, this is seen most clearly in surviving medieval timber buildings, the earliest of which use 'cruck' construction. This type of frame has no load-bearing walls, and the whole weight of the roof is carried to earth by a framework of curved timbers, called crucks. In the late Middle Ages, braced timber framing was used, where the strength lies in the frame. The materials that fill the space between the timbers, such as wattle and daub (clay mixed with straw spread onto wooden laths)

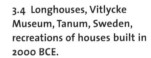

3.4 Longhouses, Vitlycke
Museum, Tanum, Sweden,
recreations of houses built in
2000 BCE.

covered with plaster, only keep out the weather. In some framed buildings, the timbers are deliberately exposed for effect – seen, for example, at Little Moreton Hall, Cheshire, of 1559. Here the beams form diamond and quatrefoil patterns on the exterior walls; painted black, they contrast severely with the white-painted infill. Some vernacular buildings consist more of roof structure than walls. The longhouses at the Vitlycke Museum at Tanum in Sweden – recreations of Bronze Age dwellings – have thatched roofs on pitched timber-frame roofs, which go down almost to the ground, and the interior room height is increased by digging into the earth. Similar examples existed in prehistoric northern China – when many early buildings were roofed, semi-subterranean, circular or square dwellings – and in Skara Brae in the Orkney Islands.

Some structural systems are specific to a given country. The hammer-beam roof – local to England and seen at the fourteenth-century Westminster Hall in London, where decorative carved angels hang as if holding up the roof – shows even more sophisticated technology. With this type of roof, the weight is taken on brackets instead of by tie-beams spanning wall to wall. Roofs on ancient Chinese buildings have some of the most sophisticated structures in the world. Rather than relying on trusses (triangular forms) to carry the load of the roof, the Chinese system depends on pillars, struts and beams to collect the forces via the roof purlins (horizontal beams) and bring them down to the ground. Often the eaves are extended by cantilevering the roof on clusters of brackets, creating a broad verandah. The brackets may be intricately carved and painted in bright colours, depending on the status and importance of the building.

3.5 Westminster Hall, London, rebuilt 1394–1402 Henry Yevele.

Hammer-beam roof by master carpenter Hugh Herland.

Building up

Although many ingenious structures have been developed, there are some basic principles in the so-called 'fight against gravity', which determine what can be built. In building, the main forces are compression, or crushing force, and tension, or stretching force. To achieve balance, equilibrium must exist between these two forces. Compression exists in load-bearing walls, where downward pressure keeps the stones or bricks in place. This can be seen in the thick masonry construction of the pyramids or the Aztec temples, where the stone blocks on the ground project slightly from the rest of the structure, in order to bear the weight above. Load-bearing masonry walls are strong, but can only be built up to a certain height, after which they tend to become unsafe. But it is surprising just how high a load-bearing wall can be built. Some of the highest and thinnest surviving ones built of brick, now both leaning, are the 97-metre Asinelli Tower and 48-metre Garisenda Tower in Bologna, Italy, which have stood since the twelfth century. There were at one time some 180 towers in the city, built as defence lookout towers as well as status symbols for rival Bolognese noble families.

The best way of building high is to use a frame, the other basic form of construction. This concentrates the compressive forces in slender members. The frame method can be made of many kinds of materials including timber, concrete or steel. The use of a frame in building may be understood by thinking of the structure as the human skeleton, and the cladding as the skin of a person. New York's Empire State Building of 1929–31 was built using a steel frame, which is lighter and much stronger than stone walls. The frame was clad with metal panels, stone and glass and, until 1972, it had the distinction of being the tallest building in the world. Because it was built this way, it also entered the record books for the rapidity of its construction.

As has been mentioned already, the cladding of a framed building acts as an infill. Up until the seventeenth century in Britain, wattle and daub was used for this purpose in timber-framed buildings, whereas in the Far East woven reed was most often used. The Willis Faber Dumas Building in Ipswich, an office building built in 1975, uses darkened glass panels as its cladding (*see plate 2.4*). This technique is known as curtain walling, where the walls are not structural but simply hung from the steel framework.

3.6 Asinelli and Garisenda Towers, Bologna, Italy, 1109–19.

RIBA Library Photographs Collection.

3.7 Empire State Building, New York City, USA, 1929–31. Shreve, Lamb and Harmon.

RIBA Library Photographs Collection/Robert Elwall.

SPANNING SPACE

Rob Wilson

In architecture, timber, masonry or steel are used to span and enclose space in order to create sheltered and protected environments for many different functions. Some buildings also express these functions through their structural form. The development of mass societies has created a need for ever-larger structures, with greater spans and more flexible spaces for increasingly complex activities.

Buildings are under a constant series of stresses or loads that need to be in balance in order for them to stay up. The greatest and most constant of these loads, in common with all other objects on the planet, is that of gravity – a building has to support the weight of its own structure.

Traditional building materials, such as stone or brick, act well in compressive loading – when they are being pushed together. They form structures by being stacked up, channelling the load to the ground. But these materials are inefficient under tensile loading, which causes them to be forced or pulled apart – as when a weight is applied to a wire. In particular, the stresses set up by their own weight mean that they can only be used to span quite modest distances horizontally.

Gaudí, at the Expiatory Church of the Sagrada Familia in Barcelona, pushed the use of stone and masonry to extremes in an attempt to make the load-bearing walls and columns as fine and sinuous as possible. He based the forms of the masonry structure on catenary arches – which follow the curve formed by a hanging chain, which automatically assumes the shape it needs to maintain equilibrium. He did not calculate the dimensions of the church by using mechanics but by building models using chains, inverting them and then replicating their forms as closely as possible in the masonry construction. But the result, though spectacular, is still that of a forest of columns with relatively short spans between them – the sense of space is primarily vertical, not horizontal.

In fact the increasing demand for larger, free-span spaces could only be met by the development of materials such as steel and reinforced concrete. These materials are significantly stronger than brick or stone, particularly under tensile loading.

Initially these materials were used only for the framework of buildings, enabling the structure to be lighter and more open-plan. The façades were often still clad in masonry, to appear like traditional structures. It was only with the work of such designers as Frei Otto that the tensile strength of these materials was fully explored and tested. In his design for the Munich Olympic stadium in 1972, anchored steel pylons are supported by a series of wires, from which in turn a 34,500-square-metre roof hangs – formed of a steel net, infilled with acrylic glass panels. In the original competition model, Otto used a lady's stocking to simulate this roof form.

These bespoke structures, although structurally highly efficient, are both enormously expensive to construct and functionally very specific. Many activities, however, need a structure that is cheap to construct and quick to erect – and that offers a large clear neutral space or one that can be adapted easily to different functions. The development of the space frame, a three-dimensional prefabricated truss, provided this. Working in a similar way to a solid beam,

3.8 (far left) Model of interior of the Expiatory Church of the Sagrada Familia, Barcelona, Spain, 1925. Antoní Gaudí.

3.9 (left) Olympic Games Stadium, Munich, Germany, 1972. Frei Otto and Günther Behnisch.

these trusses are formed of simple elements each under simultaneous compression or tension – that is, in equilibrium. Very economical structures can be formed by directly following the lines of force that are internal to the structure. They can then be covered in a much lighter cladding material. The Sainsbury Centre for the Visual Arts (1978) at the University of East Anglia uses huge space-frame trusses. Within this single clear-span structure, glazed at both ends, a series of different functions – from an exhibition space to reading rooms and a public café – are provided. All the services are situated within the depth of the walls and the roof trusses.

More recently, the stiffness made possible through frames or grids has been exploited using materials traditionally seen as too weak to form large open structures. Shigeru Ban's Japan Pavilion at the Hanover Expo (2000) was a lattice gridshell with reinforcement provided by 440 cardboard tubes, each 20 metres long and covered by a fire-proof paper membrane with glass-fibre reinforcement.

It is formed into three undulating curves, which provide wind resistance. This structure was not only highly flexible and economical but (importantly in the context of increasingly limited resources) when dismantled at the end of the Expo, all its materials were completely recycled – even down to its sand foundations.

3.10 (below) The Sainsbury Centre for the Visual Arts, University of East Anglia, England, 1978. Foster Associates.

3.11 (bottom) Japan Pavilion, Hanover Expo, Hanover, Germany, 2000. Shigeru Ban.

Building or spanning across

The post-and-beam method of building, seen in its most basic form at Stonehenge in Wiltshire, is also known as the trabeated system, meaning the use of beams in construction. The Greeks constructed monumental buildings in durable stone this way, based on earlier timber examples, now lost. The vertical members need to be thick in order to be strong, resulting in narrow openings in relation to the mass of the walls. One breathtaking example is the Hypostyle Hall at Luxor in Egypt, part of the Great Temple of Amun-Ra, built c.1312–1301 BCE.

One way of opening up the narrow spaces of the trabeated structural system was by the introduction of the cantilever. Here the forces pushing downward at one end of the horizontal beam counteract the tendency of the unsupported end of the beam to drop. A bracket projecting from a wall to support a balcony is a common example of cantilevering. Frank Lloyd Wright's 'Falling Water' at Bear Run, Pennsylvania, built in 1938, uses the principle to a remarkable degree. The entire house is cantilevered over a steep ravine, blending into the natural environment.

Trabeated systems are not able to span large distances, but arched or arcuated ones can – and with great strength, thus enlarging the scope for architecture. Simple arches can be made by corbelling, a process involving overlapping blocks until a single slab can close the gap at the top. These had appeared in Mesopotamia (now Iraq) by 3000 BCE. What is known as the 'true arch' is formed by placing wedge-shaped same-sized stones, or *voussoirs*, side by side on a support called formwork or centring. When the final stone, or keystone, is put in place the structure is self-supporting, and the formwork can be taken away. True arches, such as those of the Roman aqueduct at Segovia in Spain of the first and second centuries CE, can span large spaces because they are supported only from the sides; downward forces are pushed laterally outwards. By placing many arches together, a curved roof is formed, called a barrel or tunnel vault. Where two barrel vaults

3.13 The Hypostyle Hall, Temple of Amun-Ra, Luxor, Thebes, Egypt, c.1312–1301 BCE.

RIBA Library Photographs Collection/Luis Renau.

3.12 Falling Water, Bear Run, Pennsylvania, USA, 1938. Frank Lloyd Wright.

3.14 Roman aqueduct, Segovia, Spain, 1st and 2nd centuries CE.

RIBA Library Photographs Collection/Bernard Cox.

intersect at right angles, the roof shape formed is known as a groin vault. The Romans used this system for their public buildings – as at the Basilica of Maxentius in Rome, where three coffered concrete groined vaults roof the central nave. On either side of the nave were three bays with barrel vaulting, which can still be seen on the north side.

Pointed arches are able to carry greater loads with greater efficiency than round ones because there is no fixed ratio between their height and span: they can be built to any width and height. In Gothic architecture, based on pointed arches, the walls became less important structurally. This allowed windows to be made larger. Pointed arches create lateral thrusts that usually need to be counterbalanced by the dead weight of buttresses on the outside of the building. In the Gothic style, flying buttresses allowed the forces to be transmitted over an arch to a solid vertical; the bulk of the support was stripped away so that more light could enter the building. Most flying buttresses have heavy pinnacles on them, whose dead weight directs the thrust of forces down to the ground rather than allowing them to shear the buttress off. However, this did not always work – even buttresses were not enough to prevent Beauvais Cathedral from falling down, because the forces of the vaults had not been assessed carefully enough.

The rib-vault principle of Gothic architecture unleashed a huge range of vaulting types, culminating in the decorative fan vaulting which is a feature of the late developments of Gothic architecture in Britain. This uses inverted half-cones with concave sides, their rims touching at the top of the vault and their visible surfaces covered with tracery. It was used spectacularly at King's College Chapel, Cambridge, built from 1508 to 1515.

Roofing over buildings with circular plans presents particular problems, but perhaps the most elegant solution is the dome. Early domes, made of wood, often used techniques borrowed from ship building. Ancient Roman domes were made of brick, stone and concrete. They were formed by building many overlapping arches, all with the same centre point. The pendentives, or spherical triangles, which created the magic 'floating' dome of Hagia Sophia, allowed it to sit on a square plan rather than a circular one (*see plate 2.29*). In Persia, small arches, or squinches, were used for building arches; later their form became smaller and purely decorative. In the arcade that surrounds the Court of Lions, in the Alhambra in Granada, Spain, built in the fourteenth century, pendants were added to the squinches so that they resemble stalactites (*see plate 3.18*).

3.15 Basilica of Constantine or Maxentius, Rome, 306–30.

3.16 Chartres Cathedral, France, 1194–c.1220. Flying buttresses.

RIBA Library Photographs Collection/Eric de Maré.

3.17 King's College Chapel, Cambridge, England, about 1441. Fan-vaulted ceiling by John Wastell, 1508–15.

3.18 The Court of Lions, The Alhambra, Granada, Spain, about 1470.

3.19 The Chapel of the Holy Shroud, Turin, Italy, 1668–94. Guarino Guarini.

The building of domes was further developed in the fifteenth, sixteenth and seventeenth centuries, many being multi-shell constructions. The dome of St Paul's Cathedral, based on St Peter's in Rome and domed churches in France, is made up of two domes, one inside the other. Between them is a shaped cone of load-bearing brick, which carries the lantern at the top of the cathedral as well as its own weight and, in part by means of trusses, supports the outer dome. To counteract the forces within the cone the architect Sir Christopher Wren used an iron chain to encircle its base, to prevent it from bursting – an idea he borrowed from Filippo Brunelleschi's dome at the Cathedral in Florence, Italy, of the fifteenth century. The inner dome is supported by pendentives resting on massive stone piers, so its weight is carried down to the building's foundation.

In the seventeenth-century Chapel of the Holy Shroud, Turin, Guarino Guarini manipulated light and geometry to create a dome whose height appears much greater than it is. Here, the complex symbolic geometry of the dome is clearly expressed in the exposed ribs. In the twentieth century a further type of dome structure was developed, a subdivided icosahedral (twenty-planed) hemisphere, first by Walter Bauerfeld at Jena, Germany, in 1925. Here the dome, a by-product of the invention of the planetarium projector, was made of light steel bars and covered with a thin shell of concrete. A little later Richard Buckminster Fuller patented the same subdivided icosahedron principle, which he called the geodesic dome. Fuller's most successful dome was the United States Pavilion, designed for Expo '67 in Montreal, made of a three-dimensional frame of hexagonal and pentagonal steel tubes and covered with a skin of shaped acrylic panels (*see plate 3.21*). Further architectural developments have evolved from the basic dome structure. The Eden Project at St Austell in Cornwall, designed by Nicholas Grimshaw & Partners and opened in 2001, uses a hexagonal grid structure of tubular steel, each hexagon nine metres across (*see plate 1.19*).

3.20 Florence Cathedral, Italy, 1296. Dome by Filippo Brunelleschi 1420–36.

The first Renaissance double dome: it was built without centring, based on techniques more similar to Islamic examples than to Roman domes.

3.21 Geodesic dome, United States Pavilion, Expo' 67, Montreal, Canada, 1967. Richard Buckminster Fuller and Shoji Sadao.

Designed as an exhibition hall for an international exposition. RIBA Library Photographs Collection/Michael Hodges.

3.22 Schlumberger Research Centre, Cambridge, England, 1982–6. Michael Hopkins & Partners.

RIBA Library Photographs Collection/Alastair Hunter.

Other construction systems for buildings have developed, including the suspension principle. This was adapted from nineteenth-century bridge design by engineers like Isambard Kingdom Brunel and others. At the Olympic Halls in Tokyo, designed by Kenzo Tange, the roof is made of welded steel net slung from steel cables suspended on reinforced-concrete masts. At the time it was built, in 1964, it was the world's largest suspended roof. The building's form derives entirely from its method of construction, and the structure is clearly visible.

In the late twentieth century the tensile structure became popular, adapted from ancient tent building, in which a lightweight skin is supported by masts or frames. This type of structure is efficient for large public buildings like grandstands. At the Schlumberger Research Centre at Cambridge of 1986, by Michael Hopkins & Partners, the roof, made of fibreglass cloth, is held up by masts between steel posts. Space frames are a more complex type of structure often made of lightweight tubing and used for buildings that require large unsupported roof areas, such as airports or exhibition halls. They are made up of triangulated frames (rigid three-sided structures), constructed in three dimensions, to resist loads in any direction. Pneumatic structures have evolved from the 1960s. They depend on air pressure for their stability. The membrane or fabric, usually reinforced with steel cables, is held up by pressurizing the air in the enclosed space below it, so the cables are stressed in tension. These kinds of structures, naturally curved, can also span large distances, and are often used for sports halls and temporary buildings such as exhibition pavilions.

Services

The way a building is constructed must also take account of the services required. Today these may include plumbing, air-conditioning or lifts – but in the past they might have simply been natural ventilation and basic sanitation. Nowadays services are usually concealed inside a building so they are invisible from the exterior. But when not considered in the initial design, they are placed on the outsides of buildings, creating eyesores (or distinctive motifs, depending on your point of view), such as the air-conditioning units placed on the outside walls of individual apartments in housing blocks in New York or Hong Kong. The Lloyds Building in London, 1979–84, on the other hand, has its services purposely placed on the exterior. There is a debate as to the extent that this makes maintenance easier, and the aesthetic function that the pipework and lavatory 'pods' also serve. The use of advanced technological services has not always been entirely successful. Service systems like air-conditioning, and the widespread use of synthetic materials in buildings, has led to the late twentieth-century phenomenon of 'sick building syndrome'. Research into the physiological effects of buildings on their users, and increased numbers of cases of the ill-effects of air-conditioning, such as legionnaires' disease, has led many to question these technological 'advances' and to find alternative methods or reuse traditional ones.

Prefabrication

Many buildings are made to be movable, including medieval framed buildings. The easiest way of doing this is by combining simple constructional techniques with prefabricated components. Prefabricated buildings made of wood, and later of cast iron, were first manufactured in the early nineteenth century and shipped to all corners of the world, particularly within the British Empire. Buildings could be ordered from a catalogue, and the parts transported to be erected on site, as they still are today. The architects Ray and Charles Eames' own house at Pacific Palisades in Los Angeles was built this way in 1945–50, using standardized components from a builder's catalogue, but arranged in innovative ways.

Prefabrication is particularly useful for buildings that are temporary and movable, like exhibition buildings. One of the earliest large prefabricated buildings was the Crystal Palace, designed for the Great Exhibition of 1851. It was made of standardized iron members, wooden frames and glass panes, and assembled on site. Its prefabrication made its construction rapid – it was built in less than six months. It was demounted in 1852, and re-erected at its second home in Sydenham in 1854, in quite a different form (*see plate Intro.3*). During the twentieth century,

3.23 (above right) Lloyds of London, London, 1979–84. Richard Rogers Partnership.

3.24 Eames House, Pacific Palisades, Los Angeles, USA, 1945–50. Charles and Ray Eames.

RIBA Library Photographs Collection/Luis Renau.

prefabrication became increasingly popular for its cheapness in manufacture. During the Second World War, 'prefabs' were manufactured in the UK to provide emergency housing for families whose homes had been bombed. Intended as a temporary solution, they were cheap and could be erected quickly. The Habitat housing at Montreal, a prototype of contemporary living built for Expo'67, similarly used prefabricated units, this time stacked on top of each other, and secured by a steel cable. The cheapness of prefabricated components meant they were popular for social housing in the 1960s, as they were manufactured off site and then incorporated into the finished building. Although quick to erect, they were later blamed for creating monotonous buildings.

3.25 Habitat housing, Expo'67, Montreal, Canada, 1967. Moshe Safdie.

Materials

The designer and theorist William Morris, writing in 1891, considered that: 'the subject of Material is clearly the foundation of architecture, and perhaps one would not go very far wrong if one defined architecture as the art of building suitably with suitable material'. Like other nineteenth-century design theorists, such as A W N Pugin, he considered 'truth to materials' to be morally and ethically superior to the plethora of artificial materials that were manufactured to imitate something else. He appreciated 'primitive' building methods and thought that materials should be used appropriately depending on a building's geographical location. He recognized that in earlier times, naturally occuring building materials were used because they were simply ready to hand.

The choice of constructional technique is always dependent on material. All materials have individual inherent physical characteristics; these include durability, strength or malleability. Some have high compressive strength, that is they resist crushing, others offer better resistance in tension, that is they resist stretching. Some structures only work with certain materials. Wood, for example, is better than stone at spanning distances, but stone is stronger in compression. Materials have always been subject to regional and geographical distribution. Certain stone, like flint, is only found in certain parts of the world, and adobe or mud bricks are made in countries with abundant supplies of the raw material and plenty of sunshine to dry them. The advent of industrialization, mass manufacture and, above all, cheap transportation subsequently reduced dependence on local materials by making possible the widespread use of uniform ready-made building components. During the nineteenth century, buildings, therefore, tended to look the same. This has led to the 'globalization' of certain types of architecture.

Certain materials are better used for building vertically, in the form of a load-bearing structure. Stone, one of the predominant durable building materials since the beginning of civilization, has been used this way for centuries. Stone walls depend for their strength on the arrangement of individual stones. As stone is hard to cut and heavy, it is expensive. Its use was confined to only the most important buildings, like temples, palaces or churches. Some types of stone are softer and easier to shape than others. In Islamic architecture, red sandstone – and later marble – was crafted into screens of pierced geometric patterns, used to control light, enhance privacy and let in cool breezes. Other stones, like granite, are exceptionally strong. In the West, so-called 'random rubble' walls are built using rough field stones (stones literally found lying in fields). These are sometimes combined with squared and coursed rubble, particularly at the corners of buildings, to give added strength. In the nineteenth century, many architects imitated the building style of the Italian Renaissance, such as the Palazzo Strozzi in Florence. They admired features like the large 'rusticated' stone courses used at the base of the building, which are not smoothed off but deliberately left rough-hewn. In the USA, architects like H H Richardson similarly emphasized the strength of stone in large public buildings by using boulder masonry or random rubble, with larger blocks on the ground floor to show how sturdy his buildings were.

Ashlar, stone that has been dressed by saw and laid with fine joints, produces a smoothly finished wall. The funerary complex built by the first known architect, Imhotep, for King Zoser at Sakkâra, Egypt, in 2778 BCE, is thought to employ the first use of ashlar. Here it was used to make a stepped pyramid. Ashlar, or dressed masonry, is often only used as the outer facing of a building, because it is so costly to produce. In the medieval period, many buildings had a rubble core and ashlar on the face only; this can sometimes be seen in ruins.

3.26 Stepped pyramid, Sakkâra, Egypt, 2778 BCE. Imhotep, for King Zoser.

RIBA Library Photographs Collection/Bernard Cox.

3.27 The mud mosque of Djénné, Mali, West Africa, 13th or 14th century. Rebuilt by Ismaila Traore in 1893.

Mortar is usually required to even out the irregularities of joints in masonry. However, at the pyramids at Giza in Egypt, and at Cuzco in Peru, the capital city of the Incas, the stones are so carefully fitted together, having been rubbed with sand (Incas did not have metal tools), that there is no need for mortar.

Individual stones for building are either found lying on the land, or may have to be quarried in blocks. Despite their weight, they can be transported long distances. Historians are still uncertain how the large blue stones were brought from South Wales to Wiltshire to build Stonehenge in the Bronze Age. The Caen stone used for parts of the White Tower at the Tower of London in the twelfth century, and at Canterbury Cathedral, was imported from Normandy ready worked, as there is no stone near London. It was also easier to transport the stone by water than from indigenous quarries, and the Norman masons were familiar with the stone. Different stones have various qualities, and uses. Granite, for example, is extremely hard and thus not easy to shape. It was used in ancient Egypt to build temples or tombs. In Britain its hard-wearing properties have made it ideal for kerb stones, cobbles and gutters. Over the centuries building technologies with stone have also developed; in ancient Egypt, it is thought that stone was cut by first making trenches in the surface, and driving in wedges of wood which were soaked in water until they expanded, cracking the stone.

Like stone, mud has been used in the form of load-bearing structures. It too is one of the earliest and most important building materials, widely distributed over the whole globe. It was used originally as mortar, to bond stones together to give stability and watertightness. In its most basic form, it can be mixed together with straw to make various building materials. In Britain it was used to make cob buildings, constructed of courses of mud mixed with chopped straw, and layers of long straw as bonding. Each course was left to dry before another was placed on top, then the whole wall was faced with plaster or limewash. Clay and straw are also used to make the filling material wattle and daub. The wattle often consisted of hazel rods, called hurdles, fixed into the horizontal members of the frame with twigs woven in and out of them, whilst the daub was a mixture of clay and chopped straw applied on both sides of the wall. In many parts of the world building with pisé, or rammed earth, has continued for centuries. It is made in wooden shutter-boards but is quicker to erect than cob because it is dry worked. In wartime, and whenever there is a shortage of materials, architects have used stabilized earth (pisé with cement) as an alternative building material.

Mud or clay, made into bricks and sun-dried, has also been used, especially in areas with a local shortage of stone and wood. It is best used for load-bearing walls, or for post-and-lintel structures. The bricks are made by pressing the mud into lumps, then dried in the air and sun and laid in courses set in mud mortar. This type of brick was used to build the ziggurat at Ur, in present-day Iraq, in *c.*2100 BCE – a stepped pyramid with ceremonial staircases on either side. In ancient Egypt, models of 'soul houses' have been found in tombs, suggesting that the typical dwelling was made of mud brick. Adobe, or unburnt sun-dried brick reinforced with chopped straw, is still used as a cheap building material for pueblos in the southern United States and Mexico; its colour and texture gives the buildings a distinctive regional look. In West Africa, mud is also used to make sun-dried bricks. The mosque at Djénné in Mali has walls of mud brick which are very thick, allowing the building to stay cool.

A refinement of sun drying is kiln-baking or firing of bricks. The Romans used kiln-baked bricks in most of their buildings, made in moulds by hand. These bricks are broad and flat compared with modern bricks, and were originally only used by the Romans as bonding courses between layers of stone masonry. Although the Romans introduced bricks into Britain, the skill of brick making was lost until centuries after the Roman occupation. They were later reintroduced when bricks from the Netherlands were imported into East Anglia in the thirteenth century, as ballast in ships, and later copied locally. In Britain in the Tudor period, bricks were used to create exceptional ornamented shapes like crow-stepped gables and chimney stacks. Bonding, the manner in which the bricks are arranged, has been used for both decorative and structural effect. The English bond (alternate courses of headers, the smallest face of the brick, and stretchers, the longer side) gradually gave way to the Flemish bond (alternate headers and stretchers in the same course) in the seventeenth century. The cavity wall, introduced in the late nineteenth century to aid insulation and damp-proofing, favoured stretcher bond, partly because it was more economical; the proportion of stretchers was greater, so fewer facing bricks are required.

In the nineteenth century, brick became the most popular building material in the West. Standardization of sizes meant that they were easier to handle, leading to speedier constructional methods. Cheap, mass produced and fire resistant, they were transported by railway to places with no tradition of brick building. This meant that buildings gradually lost their regional traits, and began to look the same wherever they were.

As well as having structural properties, bricks can have decorative qualities too. One method of making buildings different from each other was to use polychrome brickwork, employing different-coloured bricks to make multi-patterned walls. William Butterfield used such a technique at All Saints' Church, Margaret Street in London, built between 1849 and 1859. In Britain, the tradition of making patterns in brickwork continued into the twentieth century. Some local authority housing used vernacular motifs such as bricks to date the building; others used traditional structures like the crinkle-crankle wall, a continuously curving single brick wall, to give identity to housing estates. Further developments in brick making in the nineteenth century include glazed bricks, favoured for their hygienic easy-to-clean qualities. They were often used at the rears of buildings or in basement areas, partly because their glossy surfaces reflected light back into the buildings.

3.28 All Saints' Church, Margaret Street, London, 1849–59. William Butterfield.

RIBA Library Photographs Collection/Pawel Libera.

The technique of reinforced concrete was taken to artistic levels and used to spectacular effect in the construction of the Palazzetto dello Sport by the engineer Pier Luigi Nervi in Rome, completed for the Olympic Games in 1960. Here a thin concrete shell, made up of 19 precast steel-reinforced concrete panels, was placed over a sports arena. Thirty-six Y-shaped posts support the edge of the roof, transferring the weight to a ring beam underground. Prestressed concrete, developed in the 1930s, was a further development of this useful material. Prestressing gives the concrete on the tension side of a beam a compressive force of any desired magnitude. This is done by means of high-tensile steel wires which are stretched by jacks. With this fine-tuning of stresses and strength, prestressed units are stronger than non-prestressed elements.

It was not until the Industrial Revolution that iron or steel was used to a large extent in building. Until then, iron had been used as hidden cramps (metal bars with bent ends) or to strengthen wooden trusses that supported the framework of a roof. In the early eighteenth century a method of smelting iron with coal or coke rather than wood was developed by Abraham Darby in England. This meant cast iron could be produced in greater quantities and more cheaply than before. The first use of iron as a support material in bridge building, at Ironbridge, Coalbrookdale, in Shropshire, showed that a large span could be achieved with relatively little weight of structure. As iron was adapted from industrial to domestic use, architects were encouraged to use the material more widely, in roof structures, balconies and staircases. It was used at first as a form of applied historical decoration, such as the Gothic decorated arches at the train shed of Paddington Station, but later it suggested new architectural forms. Its main advantage over masonry was its economy and high strength-to-weight ratio. In the eighteenth century the different qualities of various types of iron were first recognized. Wrought iron is pliable but not very strong, whereas cast iron is brittle but has a high compressive strength. Soon wrought-iron beams were used in conjunction with cast-iron columns, for example in nineteenth century mills and factories in Britain and North America, which required large open expanses for rows of machinery. Art Nouveau architecture showed a fascination with fine ironwork, especially wrought iron. Victor Horta was one of the first architects to exploit its structural and decorative qualities, at the Tassel House, Brussels (1892–3), using it for balustrades and columns in the form of tendrils and vegetal shapes. This was one of the first instances of the use of exposed iron in a private residence.

3.35 Construction of the Palazzetto dello Sport, Rome, 1957. Pier Luigi Nervi.

RIBA Library Photographs Collection.

3.36 Tassel House, Brussels, 1892–3. Victor Horta.

Steel as a building material was costly until Henry Bessemer found a new process for its manufacture in 1856. This involved converting pig-iron into steel by blowing air through molten iron. Steel transformed architectural design by making new forms, including skyscrapers, possible. The first skyscrapers were built in Chicago, following the earthquake and fire of 1871. A group of Chicago architects exploited steel-frame construction to bring about a technological revolution in architecture, particularly using its lightweight, fire-resistant qualities. The development of the elevator by Eli Otis in the 1850s, a key invention, also aided the evolution of tall buildings. But most buildings did not show their steel frames, partly because in some places building regulations required that external walls should carry their own weight. In the United States, however, this was not a concern. The Carson Pirie Scott Store in Chicago of 1899–1904, designed by Louis Sullivan, is considered to be a pioneer of the twentieth-century office building, in which the frame dictates its form. Here, white tiles are hung on the steel frame, with a repeated pattern of windows on the upper floors and a screen of bronze and glass that serves as a store front on the ground floor. By itself, steel forms a strong structure but its behaviour in fire is unpredictable. It does not burn, but may buckle and collapse. Therefore all steel structures have to be covered with a fire-retardant substance, usually sprayed-on concrete.

3.37 Carson Pirie Scott Store, Chicago, USA, 1899–1904. Louis Sullivan.

3.38 Turbine Hall, Berlin, 1909. Peter Behrens for AEG.

RIBA Library Photographs Collection/Julian Osley.

3.39 Hong Kong & Shanghai Bank, Hong Kong, 1979–86. Foster Associates.

The high-rise steel frame has subsequently been refined. To resist wind-loading, many have a stiff core, cross-walls and a braced outer skin, so that the building can move slightly. The Hong Kong & Shanghai Bank in Hong Kong, by Foster Associates, of 1979–86, exposes a framework which appears to be load bearing although it is part of the lateral wind-stiffness system. Other tall buildings, such as the John Hancock Center in Chicago, transfer loads to steel corner columns in addition to having steel members in the form of cross-bracing.

Steel-frame construction did not transform all architecture suddenly, and in many cases steel-framed buildings were made to look like traditional load-bearing structures. Peter Behrens's Turbine Hall for AEG in Berlin, of 1909, uses cranked (elbow-shaped) steel trusses that support the roof and cladding of the building, and also the rails of two 50-tonne gantry cranes. But on the façade he added heavy concrete corners to the frame, which slope in gradually as if to hold an invisible classical pediment; this gives the exterior its monumentality.

3.40 Maison de Verre, Paris, 1928–32. Pierre Chareau and Bernard Bijvoet.

3.41 Institut du Monde Arabe, Paris, 1981–7. Jean Nouvel.

Detail of south façade showing diaphragm shutters from the inside. RIBA Library Photographs Collection/Roy Herman Kantorowich.

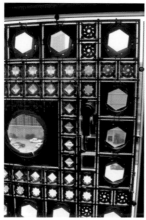

Glass has been used as a building material in a number of innovative, non-structural ways. Improvements in glass making coincided with architectural developments. Early glass was handmade and consequently expensive. It was usually leaded (cut and placed in lead surrounds) and used for important buildings as in the large rose and lancet windows in Gothic churches and cathedrals. As glass manufacture was mechanized in the nineteenth century, it became possible to make larger sheets of glass more economically. The cylinder method of making flat glass was improved to make broad or sheet glass. As taxes on glass were abolished, in Britain in the mid-nineteenth century, the use of large sheets of plate glass became feasible. Used together with iron, glass was ideal for industrial buildings that required large window areas, such as railway station roofs, exhibition halls and gallerias. In the twentieth century, glass has been used adventurously for its light-transmitting and reflecting qualities, for example in the 1920s as glass-brick walls at the Maison de Verre in Paris, by Pierre Chareau and Bernard Bijvoet. Today, glass is used for cladding – especially as curtain walling in steel-framed buildings. An exciting development has been 'smart' glass, so-called because it allows glass façades to respond dynamically to heat and light. At the Institut du Monde Arabe in Paris, by Jean Nouvel, 1981–7, the thick glass panels on the south façade have mechanized light filters or diaphragms, which open or close depending on the strength of the sun, like the lens of a camera. The façade acts as a screen, an interpretation of Arabic *mushrabiyahs*, or pierced panels. Making references to the buildings' client, the architect cleverly sought to mix Western technology with the patterning and geometry of traditional Arabic decoration, made by the diaphragms.

Plastics, like glass, have also made enormous advances as building materials, in the form of acrylic, fibreglass or polystyrene. One of the earliest experiments in the use of plastics for building was Alison and Peter Smithson's House of the Future at the Ideal Home Exhibition of 1956. This was a prototype for design for living 25 years hence. Moulded out of plastic-impregnated plaster, the house had a skin structure, the floor, walls and ceiling forming a continuous surface. The interior, with its round-edged built-in units and plastic chairs, had a sculptural, organic feel.

New forms of plastic are continually being developed. As an alternative to glass, a new transparent cladding material, ETFE (ethyltetrafluoroethylene), was developed at the end of the twentieth century – its lightweight qualities were used for the biomes of the Eden Project in Cornwall, a hexagonal-grid structure clad with inflated ETFE cushions (*see plate 1.19*). In addition to insulating the domes (the three layers of foil have air between them), it is a transparent recyclable material, not degraded by daylight.

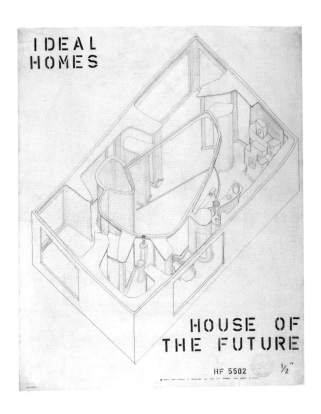

3.42 Design for the House of the Future, Ideal Home Exhibition, 1956. Alison and Peter Smithson.

An axonometric drawing that shows the plan and elevations in the same drawing. Pencil on tracing paper. V&A: E 663–1978.

Materials and techniques developed in other industries

Plastics were first used in product design before being developed as a constructional and engineering material. Many building materials and construction techniques were first developed in other forms of manufacture, such as the aircraft industry, and later adapted for use in building. Wartime conditions also boost technology and mass production; afterwards alternative uses for certain materials are found, or methods of manufacture adapted to the production of building materials. The American inventor and architect Buckminster Fuller sought to adopt the mass-production techniques of the motor industry as the model for building houses. His Dymaxion House, designed in 1945 as a low-cost residence that could be dismantled and moved, used surplus aluminium from the aircraft industry. The house was even to be mass produced by an aeroplane manufacturer, the Beech Aircraft Company of Wichita, Kansas. Many Modern Movement houses used features borrowed from other industries, for example the flats at Avenue de Versailles in Paris, by Lubetkin and Ginsberg of 1928–31, used handles and window mechanisms taken from the car industry.

Building structures have also been adapted from other fields. The wooden frame of the aeroplane the Vickers Wellington was invented by Barnes Wallis just before the Second World War. Called a gridshell, this is a structure with the shape and strength of a double-curvature shell, but made of a grid instead of a solid surface. Edward Cullinan Architects used the structure in the form of a diagonal grid of oak laths when designing the Downland Gridshell, completed in 2002, a store and workshop for the Weald and Downland

3.45 Page from the Book of St Albans, about 1250.

This page shows the building of St Albans abbey church.

The building process in the Middle Ages, sometimes illustrated on medieval illuminated manuscripts, used the basic sources of power and technology then available. Often the master mason, when shown, holds a pair of dividers used for setting out the work, rather than drawings. By the fourteenth century, craftsmen, whether glass makers, plumbers or brick layers, had formed guilds relating to their trade, based on mutual aid. These limited the number of people who could be trained in a trade in a certain area, making sure knowledge was retained within a closed group. Their guild-halls, often ornate showplaces of their craft, were used as meeting places.

In East Asia the building industry was controlled earlier than in the West. The oldest Eastern building manual, written to control building practice across the empire, and which summarized the knowledge of the day and established standards for new buildings, was the Chinese 'Yingzao Fashi' (the State Building Standards), written by Li Chieh in 1103. As well as establishing standards for tile and brick making, it also laid down a module for the size and spacing of pillars and beams.

In the West, a division between the role of the builder and designer began to emerge in about 1500, as the architect displaced much of the mason's former design role. After about 1750, as buildings became more technically complicated, the two roles of designing and building diverged more strongly.

It is perhaps not surprising to learn that the term 'architect' is derived from the Greek word '*architekton*' meaning 'builder in chief'. We know about some early Greek architects, whose role involved organizing building work but also providing schedules of measurement and full-size templates for the craftsmen. Examples include Kallikrates, active c.450 BCE and Iktinos who, between 448 and 437 BCE, constructed the Parthenon. The Roman architect Marcus Vitruvius Pollio wrote his treatise *De re archittura in libri decem* in the first century. This became the most influential architectural manual ever produced. Rediscovered and published in many versions in the Renaissance period and after, it established the principle that architecture had a theory that architects should study. The idea of establishing principles led to many other reference manuals being published in Italy and elsewhere. John Shute's *The first and chief grounds of architecture: used in all the ancient and famous monuments*, 1563, was used as a guide to the classical Orders and contained the earliest architectural intaglio plates to be published in Britain. With the invention of new scientific instruments like the camera obscura, pictorial perspective was developed in Italy in the fifteenth century. Leon Battista Alberti's treatise on architecture, *De re aedificatoria in libri decem*, published in 1483, however, advised architects against using perspective drawing because of its tendency to distort, and recommended instead the use of the ground plan and model. Alberti was one of the first to draw a distinction between the intellectual process of design and the physical task of construction.

In this period, 'architects' came to architecture indirectly. Their typical background might be theatre (Inigo Jones) or military engineering (Sébastien le Prestre de Vauban). Andrea Palladio trained as a sculptor and stonemason before being selected for further education, whilst Christopher Wren, a founder member of the Royal Society, was a mathematician and astronomer. Architecture gradually became a gentlemanly hobby, even practised by the nobility, as in the case of Lord Burlington, an amateur architect.

In the sixteenth and seventeenth centuries, architects had no formal training. They were either apprenticed, or were pupils or assistants in an architect's office. In some cases they came from being a Clerk of Works, or had trained as a mason or carpenter. Their informal training was sometimes under the wing of an enlightened patron, who they may have accompanied on the Grand Tour. It is said that Burlington's benevolence may have made it possible for Isaac Ware to visit Italy as a young man. In the eighteenth century, the study of architecture became institutionalized with the setting up of academies, often under royal patronage, which supplemented practical apprenticeship. There was always a cross-pollination of architectural ideas. In the Renaissance period, there was reliance on examples from an earlier period, particularly Roman. The results of exploration and trade in the eighteenth century encouraged architects and other designers to imitate exotic styles from far away. The Pagoda at Kew Gardens by William Chambers was built after his travels in China, where he had seen such buildings first hand (*see plate 2.47*). In the first half of the twentieth century, a number of European Modern Movement architects travelled to Scandinavia to study social housing, and brought back ideas to their native countries.

Not all architecture has been well understood. In the early nineteenth century, there was much debate about whether ancient Greek building used colour, and shock when it was discovered that this was indeed

3.46 Portrait of Isaac Ware and his daughter, about 1754. Andrea Soldi.

The architect holds his design for Wrotham Park, Middlesex, designed for Admiral Byng. Part of one of the pavilions of the house can be seen under construction beyond. He stands next to Mary Ware, believed to be his youngest daughter. Oil on canvas. RIBA Library Drawings Collection.

CHANGING TOOLS OF THE DESIGN PROCESS

Neil Bingham

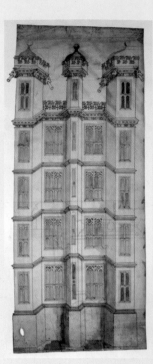

In the last few decades, the use of computers as the principal design tool in architects' offices has spelled the near-demise of the long and venerable tradition of drawing instruments. The innovative developments in computer-aided design (CAD) programmes are but the latest tools of the trade for helping architects create drawings that are accurate, easily understood and often beautiful.

Drawing instruments have changed very little in function or appearance since the ancient world, although they have become more sophisticated with time. A set of bronze instruments found in the ruins of Pompeii, buried by volcanic eruption in 79 CE, included a pen for drawing with ink, dividers for marking off distances and compasses for making circles.

During the early Middle Ages, from about 330 to 660 CE, Islamic mathematicians refined drawing instruments, so as to be more accurate for their calculations. By the age of the great Gothic cathedrals of the twelfth to fifteenth centuries, masons and carpenters required very exacting design tools to set out window tracery and roof vaults.

In the fifteenth century, during the Renaissance, architects began to refine the art of architectural drawing – aided by such discoveries as perspective, giving the illusion of objects in depth. The use of plans, elevations and details became standardized. And the preparation of sets of drawings was made easier as paper became more readily available. Previously, clay tablets and processed animal skins, like parchment and vellum, were all that had been available.

3.50 Design for one bay of Bishop Fox's Chantry, Winchester Cathedral, Hampshire, England, about 1528. English sixteenth century mason (perhaps Thomas Berty).

Sepia pen.
RIBA Library Drawings Collection.

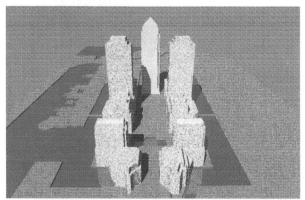

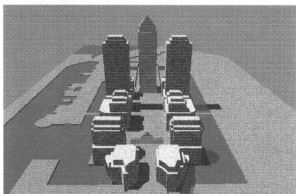

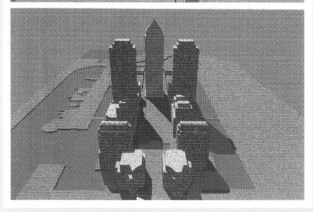

3.49 Computer-aided design study showing the effect of sunlight and shadow on Dockland Square, Canary Wharf, Tower Hamlets, London, about 1991. Skidmore Owings & Merrill.

Colour prints.
RIBA Library Drawings Collection.

3.51 *Portrait of Sir Robert Lorimer*, 1886 (detail). J H Lorimer. The architect is seated at his drawing table, leaning on a T-square and working on an architectural drawing of a wrought-iron gate.

Oil on canvas.
RIBA Library Drawings Collection.

By the early eighteenth century, sets of drawing instruments were becoming common, often made by a growing number of professional instrument-makers. Some of the makers famous in the field were the English firm of W F Stanley and the German companies of Staedtler and Faber, whose constant innovations and refinements made drawing instruments such fine and delicate working tools.

Drawing instruments are technical. Many are complex, requiring skill and dexterity. The ruling pen allowed draughtsmen to produce lines of different thickness. The pen's blades were adjusted by a little screw to vary the ink flow to the required width. But such pens were liable to clog, drip and smear, ruining a drawing and forcing the draughtsman to start all over again. The introduction of the technical pen in the 1930s, with interchangeable nibheads for lines of different widths, was a blessing for the beleaguered architect.

Each type of drawing instrument performs a specific function. To draw circles (and parts of circles) for illustrating such features as rounded windows and domes, architects used a pair of compasses. For accurately creating curves, fancy lightwood templates, called appropriately, French curves, were used.

Other methods of turning or bending a line required instruments that were sometimes traditional, sometimes novel. Set squares, for making right angles, were based upon the standard timber squares used by carpenters and the iron squares of stonemasons. Elliptographs were complicated little gadgets invented in the early nineteenth century to plot ovals. And, as fashion changed in architectural drawing, certain instruments became common. Led by architects such as Le Corbusier, for example, numbering and lettering using stencils was considered a very clean and modern look in the twentieth century.

The great improvement to the T-square and the introduction of the inclined drawing table, or board, helped to revolutionize architectural practice, beginning in the mid-nineteenth century. The T-square became a standard office instrument, its long mahogany arm gliding across the surface of the drawing, making true straight lines and aiding in keeping other instruments in place.

One of the principal occupations of many architects in large offices was to make copy drawings to be sent to clients, builders, contractors, and to the authorities for approval. For several centuries before the Victorian period, drawings were copied by the slow and laborious method known as pricking through. By laying a blank sheet of paper under the original finished drawing, and using a pin-like instrument – the pricker – the copyist pierced both sheets at strategic points of the original. The tiny holes made on the blank sheet were then joined together in ink line to imitate the original.

Early in the eighteenth century, architects began to trace drawings using paper that had been rubbed or soaked in oil, usually linseed, rendering the sheets semi-translucent. Natural tracing paper emerged in the twentieth century, using selected timber fibres beaten to a transparent appearance – but by then the photographic blueprint process was in general use for copies.

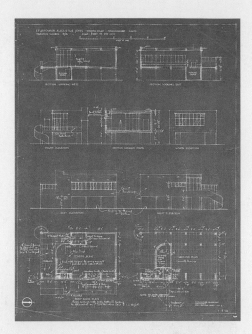

3.52 Design for Augustus John's studio, Freyn Court, Fordingbridge, Hampshire, England, about 1934. Christopher Nicholson.

Blueprint.
RIBA Library Drawings Collection.

3.53 A case of drawing instruments, belonging to Thomas Farnolls Pritchard (1723–77), made in about 1760, containing dividers, ruling pens, and a scale rule. Travelling sets such as this one were particularly useful for architects working away from the office.

RIBA Library Drawings Collection.

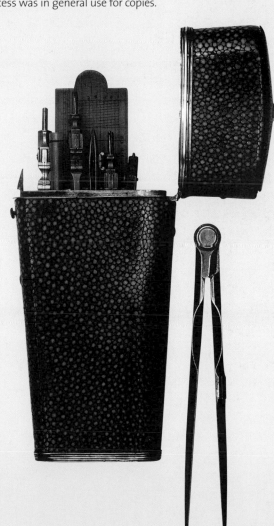

But the issue became more significant during the Modern Movement period, when architects took on the role of designing a new society. In the post-war period, one of the main criticisms of modern architecture was the extent to which the architect was divorced from the client. To prove that this was not the case, one architect, the Hungarian émigré Ernö Goldfinger, stayed in one of his new tower blocks, designed in 1967 for a London borough, for three weeks in order to convince sceptics of the pleasures of tower block life. He then returned to his own home in low-rise leafy Hampstead.

The image of the architect has changed considerably over time. This is partly due to the debate that arose in the nineteenth century on the question of whether architecture is an art or a profession. As the architectural profession grew, a stereotype of the architect emerged, partly due to the self-publicity of architects like Frank Lloyd Wright, whose autobiography was published in 1932. His pupils treated him with great reverence, seeing in him a man of enormous vision and talent. As one leading writer has said, however, the cult of the hero and the 'individualism' of the architect sat uneasily with the increasing role of partnerships in the architectural profession. The question of whether one person is responsible for a design, or whether it is the work of a team of people, is a current debate.

Partnerships, relationships and dialogues

In the West, many people are involved in putting up a building today, including construction workers, engineers, architects, project managers and developers. The way that ideas are communicated between them are continually being updated. The role of an architect today, if one is used, is often that of an overseer who coordinates the design and construction, liaising with team members. Management and organizational skills are required as often as creative skills. Apart from creative energy, architects increasingly have to have good business acumen, for instance when dealing with building or employment contracts, and to work within cost constraints. Different people in a firm are employed for their specialized skills; some may be better at the business side than at designing, others have the social skills required for finding and charming clients. In the turbulent economic conditions of today, architects have reverted to some of the roles of their eighteenth-century counterparts, taking on the jobs of the entrepreneur or developer in order to stay ahead. Sound business acumen, skills learnt or brought in by using consultants, are therefore becoming more and more widespread.

At the end of the twentieth century design-build emerged, a type of building management and new form of contracting services. With design-build, one company not only designs but also constructs the project. In Britain, some construction companies have always employed architects on a salary to provide them with designs, and much of this building work is speculative. Design-build is generally disliked by architects, who believe that it uses design in a superficial way, in the pursuit of profit.

Many architects have worked closely with builders and developers. In the nineteenth century, construction companies began to specialize in a particular building type or technique, for example house-building. This period also saw the first emergence of large building contractors who carried out the whole work, from design to completion. In Britain one such company, founded by Thomas Cubitt, achieved high status by the 1860s, having designed and built most of the fashionable London district of Belgravia in the mid-nineteenth century, as well as Osborne House for Queen Victoria on the Isle of Wight – designed in conjunction with Prince Albert. As operations on site became increasingly mechanized, builders had to learn new technologies, structures and materials. Many builders also employed architects directly, for example to produce catalogues of house plans, from which homes could be ordered directly by the customers.

Building has always involved an understanding of structures and materials, a role which engineers have increasingly taken on. Associated with inventions in the ancient Greek and Roman periods, their work expanded in the medieval period with the need for power technology to assist building works, based on water, wind and horsepower. In the West, an unprecedented demand for engineering skills followed the growth of industrial production and the need for new transport methods, such as canals. Civil engineers subsequently formed their own professional society in the late eighteenth century. For specialized structures like bridges, they worked closely with builders, integrating science and technology, but usually remained distanced from architects. In many instances in the nineteenth century, the two professions were considered separate. At St Pancras Station in London, built in the 1860s–70s, the engineers, Barlow and Ordish were responsible for designing the functional train shed, whilst the architect Sir George Gilbert Scott designed the Midland Grand Hotel in front of the shed.

Many new structures created by engineers, such as the Eiffel Tower, designed for the 1889 World's Fair in Paris, persuaded architects to consider new forms. Nowadays, architects and engineers may work closely together as a team, acknowledging each other's skills. Larger buildings necessarily require more engineering input than smaller ones. The role of the engineer has become more important as new materials are developed, allowing new constructional techniques. The building of Sydney Opera House, designed by Jørn Utzon, began before the structure had been worked out, and thus demanded a high – but belated – engineering input. The engineers Ove Arup & Partners worked on the project from 1958. To find a solution to the construction of the roofs they experimented with precast concrete technology. Eventually a solution was found based on a sphere of fixed diameter. Sections from the sphere were taken in which only the length of arc differed (*see plate Intro.1*).

3.54 Midland Grand Hotel, St Pancras railway station, London, 1865-74. Sir George Gilbert Scott. Train shed, 1863. Barlow and Ordish.

Pen and wash.
RIBA Library Drawings Collection.

We have seen how architects have always taken on a managerial role, in addition to having the capacity to translate ideas into a form to be understood by others. They must usually work with a team of specialists, including builders and structural engineers, to ensure that the design and construction processes come together at the right time. It is a bit like assembling a giant jigsaw puzzle, but in three dimensions. There is usually no time or money for delays or to make mistakes, or as the saying goes, to 'go back to the drawing board'.

Some buildings are extraordinarily complex, and may take years to design and build. For example, when designing a technically complex building like a modern skyscraper, structural factors that must be taken into account include secure foundations; working out how the structure will be made; deciding if the building must be aerodynamic, thereby reducing wind load on the structure; and ensuring that the cladding is weatherproof and securely fastened, and that it will resist corrosion or pollution. The designer must also plan the location of services such as ventilation, toilets or lifts – usually hidden in the middle of the building – decide how it will be heated and cooled; ensure that it will be safe to use; decide how the building will be cleaned and maintained; and ensure that the building will cope with the local environment and climate, such as earthquakes and typhoons.

Similarly, materials have to be carefully selected, taking into account where they will be used in the building, how strong they are, how easy they are to maintain and how they will wear, where they are obtained from, how much they cost, and whether they convey the right message about the building.

Having resolved any construction problems, the architect or builder must decide the extent to which structural factors govern the building's final appearance. We have seen that in certain kinds of building, such as Gothic and high-tech architecture, the form of the building is heavily reliant on the type of structure chosen. But many other variables (such as location, context and cultural factors, discussed in the next chapter) need to be considered in determining the form of a building.

CHAPTER FOUR
BUILDINGS TOGETHER
Eleanor Gawne

4.1 Karl Marx Hof, Vienna, 1926–30. Karl Ehn.

All cities have distinctive features. We can picture the more famous ones in our minds, even if we have never visited them in person. It may be startling to realize how different they look from each other, and wonder why. Why does Venice look as it does, and why is it so different from Hong Kong? The main reason is that all groups of buildings, old and new, emerge from their location, their history and local culture. Venice, for instance, became a world power in the fourteenth century, primarily because of its location on the silk route between East Asia and Europe. Its situation helped it to become a trading and distributing centre for luxury goods. Because of its position on the water and the strength of its navy, it did not, unlike mainland Italian cities, need massive fortified walls. Originally a collection of swamps and islands, connected only by water, canals were made in the fifteenth century to serve as roads. As a port, its waterways ensured that merchandise like spices, silks and metals could be easily transported to the merchants' warehouses that lined the canals. Space was at a premium, so buildings were built as high as technology allowed. Hong Kong, too, has tall buildings (though much newer and higher ones than Venice) and is surrounded by water, but has developed into quite another type of city. It began as a small British colony in the nineteenth century, evolving into a major world centre of trade, transport, finance and tourism in the twentieth century. After the Second World War, the rapid growth of its manufacturing economy, and the corresponding increase in the population that came to work in it, led to pressure on the small amount of available land. This encouraged the building of tall high-density buildings, including corporate skyscrapers. Now symbolic of a thrusting mixed economy, this 'city aesthetic' has been copied by other rival cities in East Asia. This is perhaps where all cities are heading in the future.

4.2 Grand Canal, Venice, Italy, built from the 13th century.

The history of an area always affects the way the buildings look and how they relate to each other. This makes for variety in our villages, towns and cities. In fact, one can only appreciate why groups of buildings were built, and look like they do, if wider social, economic and political factors are taken into account. This applies as much to individual buildings, such as a house, as it does to a row of buildings in a street, a district or even to a whole city. The effect of a building, too, is modified by what it stands next to. Its overall impact depends on its relation to nearby buildings, as well as to other surroundings, whether roads, village greens, formal squares or pedestrian precincts. Sometimes buildings make assertive statements, seeming to ignore their neighbours; at other times they may politely merge together into the whole. This is a result of either an unconscious growth, where an area has developed organically, or a conscious one, dependent on the architect, town planner, ruler or city authorities. Above all, their context is based on the viewer's own cultural background and knowledge.

Built environments adapt to changing social and economic conditions. They grow rapidly when economically prosperous, and shrink in size when the boom is over. Bruges in Belgium, for example, was a world city of late medieval Europe before its relative decline due to competition from Antwerp in the sixteenth century. Bruges survives today in perfect form, untouched by recent development. But some towns appear and disappear completely almost overnight, like the gold-rush mining settlements of California, now ghost towns. If the period of prosperity was short-lived, most of the buildings may have been put up at the same time – when money was available. When this occurs, the overall environment becomes homogeneous, like in many Italian Renaissance towns. There may have been little new building after a certain period, or perhaps any new structures were put up only on the outskirts of town. Another economic reason for the appearance of any town or city is that land is more expensive in central districts than in outlying areas. There may also have been a conscious political decision to keep the centre of the city the same. It is now done for heritage reasons, but in some instances, such as heavily bombed towns of France after the Second World War, it was done for reasons of prestige. Towns like Nancy were rebuilt exactly as they were before their destruction.

Many towns and cities incorporate earlier urban schemes that may still be extant or lying just under the surface of the ground. It can be surprising to learn how much modern urban planning is based on ancient building plots and road systems. Archaeological digs or aerial photography can sometimes uncover older schemes, even whole forgotten towns and cities. These may have evolved organically, as represented by seemingly haphazard street patterns, or have been planned quite formally, with wide straight roads.

Planning

We tend to think of older cities developing over centuries, producing what initially looks like a maze of roads and buildings. But many ancient urban centres were created on a grid-plan, including Aztec and Mayan sites. Teotihuacán, near modern Mexico City, a city that probably contained a population of 100,000 within its 41 square kilometres, flourished during the first millennium CE and was laid out on a grid based on 60-metre-square city blocks. Its spacious planning also featured vast squares, canals and bridges.

Buildings are also sited according to specific cultural phenomena. In India, Hindu temples are arranged on the ground in a particular way, each building having a cosmic significance. Many ancient cities were planned according to where religious buildings were situated, and to have appropriate spaces for ritual performance. Buildings like temples were usually given prominence in the centre of a city, and aligned according to ancient custom and worship. Some cities probably grew up surrounding a sacred site.

Another ancient city based on a grid system of streets was discovered in the early twentieth century at Mohenjo-Daro on the Indus, in north-west Pakistan. This was a large city of mud-brick houses built around 2600 BCE, with high-quality water supply and drainage systems. Greek towns too were built on a grid pattern, traditionally said to have been introduced by Hippodamus of Miletus in the fourth century BCE,

4.3 View of Washington DC, USA, laid out from 1791 to 1792.

Based on a design by Pierre Charles L'Enfant.

which was later copied by the Romans. The Romans also followed the Greek idea of the city as a sequence of outdoor public rooms, with a forum (or meeting place) at its centre.

Many Chinese cities are similarly divided this way, with square areas containing houses and courtyards, and chief buildings on the central axis. The grid pattern is an economic form of plan, and it is thus ideal for reconstructing old towns or building new ones quickly. In some instances, grids have been applied to inappropriate sites, such as the hilly landscape of San Francisco.

Many towns and cities may have grown in an unselfconscious organic way, but in the Renaissance period the classical influence was demonstrated in plans of new districts within towns (as well as whole new towns) using radial and circumferential streets. In Rome in the sixteenth century, Pope Sixtus V planned to improve the city to help the flow of vast numbers of pilgrims during certain holy years, by laying out new long straight streets, and creating vistas. Similarly, at Karlsruhe in Germany, the town and park were laid out from 1715 with radial streets emanating from the castle, primarily to facilitate the King's hunting. This became the model for later great estates. In Britain and Ireland in the eighteenth century, ideas about the Roman circus or half-circus were adapted to areas of London, Bath, Dublin and Edinburgh, and led to the fashion for crescents and circuses. This kind of planning led not just to new streets, but also to buildings presented in a uniform and symmetrical way. The European method of town planning was later copied around the world, most notably in the USA. At Washington DC in the late eighteenth century, the French military engineer L'Enfant combined grid and radial systems, with diagonal avenues linking up important monuments and buildings. Sometimes this kind of formalized planning was applied to colonial cities, like New Delhi, the new capital of British India begun in 1913. Here, very low densities and wide straight roads were entirely unlike conventional Indian cities.

In the late nineteenth century, with the effects of industrialization spoiling cities, in the form of pollution and overcrowding, reformers put forward ideas for overcoming them. One proposal was to use town planning to create a moral and social order. In the US, the City Beautiful movement stressed the role of the built environment as an uplifting and civilizing influence. The idea was based on using the neo-classical style in its buildings and monuments, laid out uniformly and on imposing avenues. It was seen first at the Chicago World's Columbian Exposition of 1893, but was put into action at Washington DC in 1901 to complete L'Enfant's original plan of the 1790s. Though it created monumental spaces and grand vistas, the scale was overwhelming, and people felt swamped by its vastness. In Washington the distances are so great that, although it makes an ideal city for processions, it is not a city for pedestrians.

THE PLANNED AND THE UNPLANNED: FROM SETTLEMENTS TO CITIES

Rob Wilson

Settlements usually originate around natural features – such as a plentiful water supply, or at a natural harbour or river crossing – making them good and accessible places to live. Where a combination of these factors coincides, settlements often develop into cities. Thus most cities start as unplanned, organic entities developing irregularly in response to site conditions.

Bristol's origins are revealed by its name, which derives from the Anglo-Saxon Bricgstowe, meaning 'place of the bridge'. Founded on a well-drained raised site adjacent to a crossing point of the River Avon, the city was an important trading centre, controlling a navigable waterway at a time when good roads were rare.

Once settlements grow into cities, more complex societies develop as, with the growth of trade, they gain strategic and economic importance. They become centres of vested interest for those in power who, to maintain the status quo, often adapt the plans of cities – either to directly defend their position, or to reflect patterns of land ownership or new cultural influences.

When the Normans took power in the eleventh century, they built Bristol Castle to defend the city and its importance as a trading centre. A new moat connected the River Avon with the River Frome, effectively making the city an island. But development remained largely unplanned. Unchecked construction caused overcrowding,

necessitating extensions of the city wall and rebuilding of the old bridge to accommodate the increase in traffic.

By contrast Palma Nuova is, as its name implies, a whole city planned and built from scratch. It sits on a flat greenfield site and has broad streets radiating out from a central public square. It was built from 1593, in the Friuli district of Italy, to defend Venice's inland empire, and reflects the ideas of the architect Vincenzo Scamozzi and Renaissance theories of military defence. It is surrounded by a series of symmetrical bastions, forming a nine-sided polygon.

The growth of settlements is also linked to developments in technology, particularly communication and transport – which improve the original conditions of a site, maintaining a city's importance as a meeting place and centre for trade.

Palma Nuova's importance vanished once the power of Venice declined, hastened by the opening-up of trade routes across the Atlantic from which Bristol would grow rich. However well planned, as a single-purpose city built to defend not its own economic interests but that of another city, it is now just a quiet country town.

With industrialization from the nineteenth century onwards, cities became increasingly attractive as places of economic opportunity. Combined with developments in transport technology, which made them far more accessible, populations have risen dramatically putting increasing strain on infrastructures.

Originally the Aztec capital, founded on a series of islands in a lake and subsequently built over by the Spanish, Mexico City has seen its population increase from 100,000 to over 20 million in less than 100 years. This population explosion has led to the unregulated sprawl familiar in many contemporary cities, made worse here by the surrounding mountains that trap the city's chronic air pollution produced by the millions of cars.

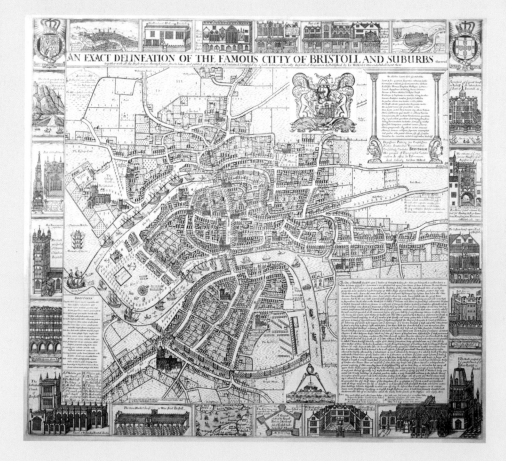

4.4 *Delineation of the City of Bristol*, 1673. James Millerd.

Engraving.

Mexico City is an example of how uncontrolled growth begins to destroy the very conditions that encouraged the initial siting of the city. Planning is often used to try and restore order and maintain these conditions. In England, attempts to limit the sprawl of London resulted in the establishment of the Green Belt and a series of satellite towns. These were designed to offer improved quality of life, more access to green open space and separation of commercial and residential areas. The last to be established, in 1967, was Milton Keynes.

Originally designed to grow over 30 years to a population of 150,000, mainly overspill from London, Milton Keynes was strategically placed midway between the capital and Birmingham on good communication routes. The loose grid of its plan, with no specific centre, defines one-kilometre squares, enabling cars to penetrate to every area of the city accessing a range of pedestrianized shopping centres as focii. Intended to avoid the problems associated with concentrically planned and zoned cities, which result in congestion towards the centre, Milton Keynes was designed around the car so as not to become a victim of it. Its strategic framework was that of a planned 'unplanned' city with the usage of areas designated in response to need over time, and not by a pre-determined zoning strategy.

Whilst many new towns have been successful, the separation of different functions, such as that of the pedestrian from the car, can result in an artificially imposed order in a city. This can stifle natural development and fail to create any sense of place. A balance is needed for a healthy city.

4.5 (top left) Palma Nuova, Veneto, Italy, 1593–1623. Vincenzo Scamozzi. Aerial view.

RIBA Library Photographs Collection/Michael Hodges.

4.6 (top) Mexico City, Mexico, founded as Tenochtitlán in 1325.

4.7 (above) *The City Centre Completion in 1990*, 1974. Helmut Jacoby. An imagined aerial view of the future Milton Keynes, Buckinghamshire, England.

Ink & watercolour spray.

Security

All settlements, ancient and modern, are the result of basic social needs. These include population growth, security, water and food, trade and communications. One of the most basic demands is the need for security. Castles, fortresses and whole cities were once fortified by thick stone walls or earth ramparts, sometimes in concentric layers, one behind the other. In some cases, the walls were surrounded by a moat, or sited adjacent to an existing river, to add a further degree of protection. In certain countries, buildings are tightly packed together to aid defence. The Taos pueblo in New Mexico, built of adobe, looks like one large building although it is made up of lots of individual dwellings. The houses originally had no front doors or windows. When there was danger of enemy attack, the owners climbed up ladders and entered through the roofs, then pulled up the ladders behind them.

Many European medieval cities were built with extensive walls around them and, as in York in England, Lucca in Italy and Montreuil in France, one can sometimes still walk around the tops of them. Renaissance fortifications were built with thick walls around their edges, enclosing wide areas of raised ground. In fact at Lucca, the bastions and tops of the walls were landscaped and planted for leisure pursuits not long after they were first built for defensive purposes. In Vienna, the glacis (the bank sloping down from the ramparts) and esplanade of the seventeenth-century fortifications were developed in the 1860s to form the

Ringstrasse – the wide street that encircles the old town, separating it from the outlying districts. Large gates were usually placed in the walls through which citizens passed, so the city authorities could check who was entering, or what goods required taxing. Some gates functioned specifically for the collecting of customs. The Brandenburg Gate, originally one of eighteen gates set into the ramparts of Berlin, was used for this purpose. The two buildings either side used to house the toll collectors, before the gate was pulled down and a new one built in 1789–93.

Many ancient Chinese cities were also walled; in Chinese the word *cheng* is synonymous for both 'walls' and 'city'. They served not only for protection, but also acted as symbols of imperial authority. In Beijing, the city's walls were moved and additional layers added over the centuries, depending on the current ruler's wishes. The fortified gates into the city had crescent-shaped bastions built, to act as further protection. In the seventeenth century, having been captured by the Manchu, the city was zoned and divided up into two areas, an Inner City for the Manchus, and an Outer City for the Chinese. The original plan of the walled city of Beijing was almost symmetrical, with the Forbidden City of the Imperial family at the centre, the best-protected part of the city, on a north-south axis. Walls caused a problem with expansion, which led to building upwards in a limited space, producing cramped and later insanitary living conditions for its inhabitants. Often the poorest citizens had to live outside the walls in shanty towns, and these areas were usually where the black-market economy thrived. Or they were the preserve of specialist trades that required large open spaces or plentiful supplies of running water, such as the textile industry.

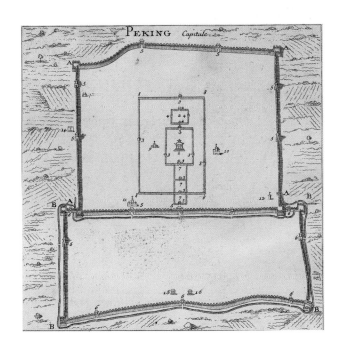

4.9 Plan of the walled city of Beijing, China, built from the 13th century CE.

In the 17th century the city was zoned, divided into an Inner City for the Manchus and an Outer City for the Chinese. Plate I, *Villes de la Province de Petche-li*', in *Description géographique, historique, chronologique, politique et physique de l'Empire de la Chine et de la Tartarie chinoise*' by J B du Halde (Paris: Lemercia, 1735)

4.10 The Brandenburg Gate, Berlin, 1789–93. C G Langhans.

The need for security within our homes has become even more of an issue today. The fear of being attacked or burgled has led to a new growth of walled or gated communities, in which electronic gates and video surveillance are intended to keep 'undesirables' out. In fact, this has echoes in Georgian developments, where visitors and tradesmen were checked by a warden (in a lodge or gatehouse) before being allowed entry to a square or street. The threat of violence and the need to feel secure has led to guarded communities in many US suburbs. This may possibly be the result of the tradition for open front lawns that reach down to the road, in a kind of 'prairie' style, with no fence to signify public and private boundaries. Anyone who has seen the small signs on many lawns which, rather than reading 'Please Keep Off the Grass', says 'Warning, Armed Response' feels alarm, and presumably this helps to deter any would-be burglars. At its most extreme, some American homeowners have built 'secure rooms' in their houses, armour-plated places of last resort from attack.

Many larger castles and forts were designed almost as mini-towns, with all the practical prerequisites needed to withstand long sieges. They were made up of specialized buildings grouped according to function, including living accommodation or barracks for soldiers, stables and pens for animals, and stores for food. Occasionally the functions spilled out of the castle, and new towns began to develop around their walls. The layouts of palaces and country houses developed from the castle. The feudal system encouraged the growth of large estates, in which the landlord kept his workers in their subservient role by forcing them to rely on him for their livelihood – living, as they did, in tied accommodation. In the eighteenth century the local nobility sometimes moved whole villages a few miles away, so as not to spoil the view from a newly built house and landscaped gardens. When rebuilt, these 'model' estate villages consisted of standardized buildings and features; often the buildings were painted the same colour so it was clear everyone knew who they belonged to.

Population

Towns and cities grow or contract depending on several factors, not least population growth. At times of major epidemics – such as the Black Death in the fourteenth century, when a quarter of Europe's population died – or during wars, places can empty quickly, and buildings become redundant (though they may be reused later for other purposes). When cities expand rapidly, as they did during the Industrial Revolution in Britain, there is often little time to plan properly, resulting in overcrowded urban areas. In places where there is a lack of housing, shanty towns are built by the incoming economic migrants. Cities have always attracted people, primarily in search of work. During the twentieth century, the populations of certain world cities rose at alarming speed. Mexico City's population, for instance, has risen from three million in 1950, to almost ten million in 1995. For most of the twentieth century, architects and planners have sought to address housing shortages by building new estates, or even whole new towns. Although population densities rise and fall naturally, planners have tried to control them by fixing on what they consider to be an ideal population size and urban density. Ideas of ideal densities have gradually fallen over time, so it is now thought that fewer people per hectare or house is better than more. However, the mid to late twentieth-century phenomenon of a falling population in the central districts of a city, has led to what is called 'densification', where population densities in existing urban areas are raised in order to rejuvenate dying centres. What has seemed impossible to take into account has been changing demographic patterns: in the West today there are more elderly people (due to improved heath care) and fewer young people (due to falling birth rates) than ever before. More people are also choosing, or being forced, to live alone. This will create a demand for more single-person and elderly households. It has also promoted the growth of retirement communities, pioneered in the USA, some of which strictly control their inhabitants' lifestyles.

For centuries, certain areas of towns and cities were designed to accommodate certain classes of society, the buildings distinguishable from the others by their size and perhaps their architectural features, such as the number of windows. In the West, in the post-war period, suburbs were criticized for their social uniformity, as places where only the middle classes lived. The residents, of course, liked them for this very thing, and they have remained the most popular places to live.

Politics

Buildings, and even whole cities, are always shaped by politics and changes in power. Some of the largest town-planning schemes have occurred under totalitarian regimes, in which planning is a product of a systematic socio-political ideology. Fascism in particular promoted not only individual buildings in a certain style, but town planning as symbolic of political power. Albert Speer's plan for Berlin of 1936, based on Roman town-planning principles (of which only the Olympic Stadium was built) was part of Adolf Hitler's desire to recreate the might of the Roman Empire. Benito Mussolini, too, harked back to Roman imperialism by excavating important areas of Imperial Rome, and rebuilding parts of the city with new roads such as the Via dei Fori Imperiali and the Via del Teatro di Marcello, both opened in 1933. Not all these 'improvements' were beneficial, particularly to those people whose homes were demolished and whose communities were disrupted to make way for the new schemes. Under the Communist leader Nicolae Ceausescu, the rebuilding programme of the Romanian capital in the 1970s and 1980s involved the destruction of a significant part of the old city of Bucharest, including many ancient Orthodox churches. This has left a peculiarly empty and lifeless centre. New buildings, such as the vast House of the People (renamed Palace of Parliament after the fall of the Communist regime) overlooking the broad but desolate central avenue, are depressingly ill-proportioned and badly detailed.

Not all idealized schemes produce such sterile environments. In nineteenth century Paris, for example, Baron Haussmann was commissioned by Napoleon III to create a series of boulevards and civic spaces, involving the demolition of hectares of medieval streets and buildings. A number of key monuments and new public buildings, such as the Paris Opera House, were incorporated into the scheme to create important vistas. Today the elegant and wide streets allow free-flowing traffic, but in fact they were

4.11 Opera House, Paris, 1861–74. Jean-Louis-Charles Garnier.

RIBA Library Photographs Collection/Emmanuel Thirard.

4.12 Medici Palace (Palazzo Riccardi), Florence, Italy, 1444. Michelozzo di Bartolommeo.

originally created so that troops could move easily around the city, and to prevent the erection of barricades. New building regulations also tied the height of cornice lines to the widths of streets and the angles of roofs, to allow daylight to reach the streets.

Some planning schemes were devised as a way of boosting the building trades in times of economic depression. President Roosevelt's 'New Deal' scheme in the USA in the 1930s was behind the setting up of the Works Progress Administration. This was responsible for much new building (thus boosting employment), including new towns, model communities and public works such as schools, hydroelectric stations and dams. Employment opportunities were again created in the 1980s, when so-called Enterprise Zones in Britain and the US were set up as an attempt to rejuvenate decayed urban centres by relaxing planning controls so that new business centres could be built rapidly and cheaply. They were often criticized for the emphasis placed on quick economic return, at the expense of architectural quality. On London's Isle of Dogs, an Enterprise Zone was created around Canary Wharf despite local opposition to the fact that there were too many office buildings and not enough local housing. Government-approved zoning also has knock-on effects on areas nearby, with derelict warehouses once used for the storage of goods reused for office or living accommodation. As once run-down areas are repopulated, new demands are generated for services such as shops, stations and bars. Districts of a city continually change and adjust according to the political climate.

Commerce

In the late Middle Ages, greater stability and growing economic prosperity boosted the status of towns. In each city of the Italian states in the fourteenth century, the civic hall on the main square or market place became the focus for city life. The main square could be used for a range of occasions including pageants, religious festivals, state processions and trade. Certain building types, such as the Florentine palazzo, were adopted as the power base for Medici and other rival wealthy families. Originally acting as symbols of self-aggrandizement, they eventually became the prototype for large urban buildings elsewhere, like clubs and offices. The growth of market towns began about this time. Traders' stalls were initially erected in the open air, usually in the central square. It made sense for traders to congregate in the same area, so that all transactions could take place there, and no prospective purchaser would be missed. Basic stalls later became more permanent buildings, first in a covered market, and later still as houses with shops on the ground floor. In some instances a market hall was erected for this purpose. In towns that specialized in a certain commodity, specific buildings were built for trading. At Ypres, which was an international centre for the cloth trade, an elaborate and impressive cloth hall was built in the thirteenth century – bigger than many cathedrals of the time – in which the annual cloth fair was held. Manufacturing and trading also encouraged the building of exchanges, where merchants could transact business in the company stock.

4.13 Cloth Hall, Ypres, Belgium, 1202–1304.

Destroyed in 1915, the present one is a replica. RIBA Library Photographs Collection.

Location and site (and spaces in between)

All buildings relate to their site, whether in a planned or unplanned way. The ancient Greeks were particularly sensitive to the relationship of their buildings to the environment. Many of their theatres used the natural landscape as a permanent architectural backdrop, and they sited their temples carefully according to how the sun moved around them. Landscaping has developed considerably over the centuries. Open public spaces, or parks, were not always considered necessary because the wealthy could afford to have a country residence and go there for their recreation. With the growth of a new middle class in Europe in the seventeenth century, who did not come from the landed gentry or have private estates to go to, private and public gardens began to be popular in the middle of towns. Large public parks were considered desirable for health reasons and were often converted from royal hunting parks, such as Hyde Park in London and the Bois de Boulogne in Paris. Some parks became vast open-air entertainment centres, where visitors could eat outside, attend dances and concerts and, in some cases, enjoy funfairs.

Central Park in New York City, laid out on land reclaimed from shanty towns by the landscape architect Frederick Law Olmsted and his partner Calvert Vaux, was the result of a competition from 1858. It followed many years of pressure from publicly minded citizens who thought Manhattan needed a park, copying European prototypes. After a vast movement of rock and soil, this 340-hectare space in the centre of the city

4.14 View of Balcony Bridge, Central Park, New York City, USA, about 1860.

Olmsted and Vaux created a picturesque landscape for the park. Vaux designed most of the 46 bridges. Albumen print. RIBA Library Photographs Collection.

was transformed into an undulating verdant landscape, with picturesque bridges and pavilions designed by Vaux. As a by-product, planning the park and moving the poor from the area had the effect of gentrifying the district, promoting the development of the upper part of Manhattan Island.

Fashions in landscaping have veered between the formal and the picturesque. The formal method was a way of controlling wilderness, by bringing architecture to gardening. The picturesque method, on the other hand, used painterly imagination to create an artificial landscape that was meant to look supremely natural. In eighteenth-century England, the picturesque method was used at country estates like Stourhead in Wiltshire, where individual buildings were grouped on a set route around an artificial lake, reminiscent of a painting by Claude Lorrain.

The picturesque tradition resurfaced in England in the 1950s, combined with Le Corbusier's ideas of siting tower blocks within a parkland in order to provide open spaces and clean air for residents. The London County Council used it when landscaping new housing estates like Roehampton in west London, called by Nikolaus Pevsner 'one of the masterpieces of post-war residential design'. Here blocks of flats, maisonettes and two-storey terraced houses are placed carefully amongst trees retained from the gardens of large Victorian houses, which had originally stood on the site. At the time, Nikolaus Pevsner claimed that 'The setting of a cubic type of building in landscape is [sic] eighteenth century tradition.' Later developments like Roehampton used tower blocks to create a landmark or vista, to be seen from a distance.

4.15 Map of the City of New York, USA, 1828. Known as the Goodrich Map.

The form that groups of buildings take is based not only on land use and zoning, but also on plot sizes and land tenure. The right or title of the land affects the kind of property that is built; it would be foolish to build a large and substantial building if the lease was too short to make any substantial profit. In newly established countries like the USA in the eighteenth century, the government offered land (originally taken from the Native Americans) to any prospective settler, and provided guarantees of rights of ownership. Similarly, the sale of land to developers around major conurbations in the 1930s led to the rise of suburbs.

The sizes of the plots of land that were originally marked up and sold off also affect the way a town or city grows. On Manhattan Island, New York City – planned on a grid pattern in 1811 (as high as 155th street) – each of the 2,028 blocks, nearly identical in dimension, was subdivided into standard lots 100 feet deep by 25 feet wide (30 metres deep by 8 metres wide). This street and building pattern has continued to the present. However, in the twentieth century some commercial enterprises broke with tradition by setting their buildings back from the street line and placing plazas in the front. The Seagram Building on Park

Avenue, completed in 1954–8, for instance, takes up only half of its site, creating a plaza open to the public. Even earlier, in the 1930s, the Rockerfeller Center was built over several blocks, with a large public space used for ice skating in the winter.

The idea of having a 'green belt', a strip of open land around an urban centre, is centuries old, and even Queen Elizabeth I tried to restrict new building within three miles of London's limits. The idea, though, particularly dominated much twentieth-century town planning. Additionally, in the late twentieth century, 'brownfield' sites – previously used for industry – were held up as key sites for development, especially as they can help rejuvenate a disused area. But they can be dangerous if the site contains industrial waste that has sunk into the ground, hidden from view. It can contaminate groundwater, or the earth on which new homes are built, and in extreme cases, harm people's health. In the latter half of the twentieth century, some outlying districts were turned into science parks. In the UK, they were formed in the 1970s to accommodate science-based industrial companies or research institutes. These were initially established near university towns, later growing into general business parks. Industrial estates have existed for much longer, areas of standardized large sheds containing light industry, warehouses, and now the ubiquitous do-it-yourself stores. Like much of suburbia, this kind of environment can feel alienating, and only comfortable to look at from inside a car.

Industralization

In the early nineteenth century, many industrial towns developed so quickly that there was little time to plan effectively. As people flocked into cities from the nearby countryside, substandard housing in rows, or back to back, was erected close to factories, so that workers were near to their places of employment. Later, multi-storey tenements were built to solve these housing problems. In New York City, tenements housed a quarter of the city's population within seven years, from being first introduced in 1901 – although one particular type, the dumb-bell plan tenement, was later condemned. These were blocks in which rooms overlooked enclosed light-wells, so that air and light were in short supply. In the twentieth century, cities that industrialized quickly – like São Paulo, the biggest city in Brazil – have similarly expanded in an uncontrolled way, due to exponential population growth. In industrialized Britain, after employment hours became formalized and recreation time was legally provided, holiday resorts emerged for workers to enjoy on their days off. Many seaside resorts developed from fishing villages from the eighteenth century onwards, and became fashionable and popular, especially when patronized by royalty.

As a reaction against the appalling conditions that nineteenth-century factory workers had to endure, some enlightened manufacturers sought to improve their employees' lives by providing model housing. This probably was not done entirely for philanthropic reasons, but was due to the realization that healthy and happy workers were more productive. In Britain in the late nineteenth century, company towns such as Saltaire and Port Sunlight were planned with plenty of amenities and open spaces. Houses at Port Sunlight were designed in a semi-rural style with large front gardens, contrasting severely with the back-to-back or terraced housing in most cities.

In the twentieth century, some model housing estates had enormous influence on the architectural scene. At the German Werkbund exhibition held in Stuttgart in 1927, a number of European Modern Movement architects were invited to design different types of housing – including villas, terraces and apartment blocks – under the direction of Mies van der Rohe. The houses of the resulting Weissenhofsiedlung estate were designed for people with middle incomes, although the ideas behind them were thought useful to other city councils grappling with their own social-housing problems. Although presented in the form of an exhibition, the houses were permanent, and they became a place of pilgrimage for budding young architects to visit. A similar model estate was built for the Austrian Werkbund exhibition in Vienna in 1930, again by a number of European architects.

4.16 Seagram Building, New York City, USA, 1954–8. Ludwig Mies van der Rohe.

Garden cities

For many people, suburbs are the ideal combination of town and country. They provide easy access to the amenities and workplaces of the city, with the open expanses of semi-countryside near to home. One of the first garden suburbs built consciously on this principle was Bedford Park, Chiswick, west of London, begun in the 1870s. Planned by William Wilson, with many buildings designed by Richard Norman Shaw, the large Queen Anne Revival houses for middle class families were arranged around a village green, with a church and public house nearby, and easy access to the city by underground railway.

Ebenezer Howard's ideas for the garden city were a reaction against the pollution and deprivation endemic in nineteenth-century city life. Published in 1898 as *Tomorrow: A Peaceful Path to Real Reform*, more commonly known by its later title *Garden Cities of Tomorrow*, his vision had a long-lasting effect on town planning. Howard's garden city diagram consisted of a central city, containing zoned areas for commercial and industrial centres, surrounded by satellite towns where the majority of the population would live. Howard's idea ensured that the area between the two – the green belt, a piece of land of farms, forests and reservoirs – had building restrictions, so that the population was never far from open land. Letchworth, in Hertfordshire, is considered to be the world's first garden city, based on Howard's principles. Founded in 1903, designed by Raymond Parker and Barry Unwin, its uniform architecture and generous planting were important to its success. More importantly, it was also run by a private company rather than by the local authority, so its inhabitants took greater pride in ensuring it was well maintained and cared for. Howard's ideas continued to be a major influence on new-town policies, especially the American green belt towns of the 1930s and the British New Town programme of the 1940s.

The idea of setting social housing amidst greenery was taken up in many German and Austrian schemes in the 1920s and 1930s. In Vienna, the Karl Marx Hof, built 1926–30 to designs by Karl Ehn, was part of the Social Democrat programme to bring socialist principles to the city's infrastructure (*see plate 4.1*). The regime's main achievement was the building of new housing blocks with communal public facilities such as laundries. The Karl Marx Hof, a showcase for 'Red Vienna', consisted of a single continuous structure over a kilometre in length, with paths and streets accessible through round-arched openings. At its centre was a large public square, and two long enclosed courtyards either side. The housing used garden-city principles applied to a single block of flats, rather than family houses, and cleverly combined public, private and communal space.

4.17 'Group of slumless, smokeless cities', representing the Social City, 1898. Ebenezer Howard. Published in *Tomorrow: A Peaceful Path to Real Reform* (known later as *Garden Cities of Tomorrow*).

Howard proposed a cluster of six garden cities – with wedge-shaped local wards, which pre-dated neighbourhood units – around a larger central city.

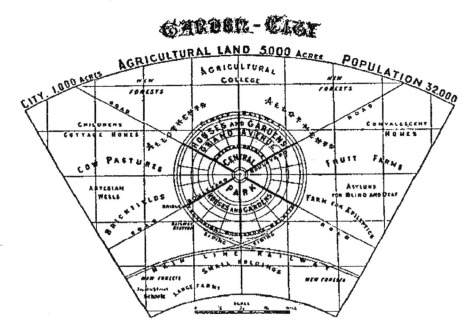

Government legislation and rules

If we compare a city like Los Angeles, which has had relatively little planning control, with one like London, it is obvious that the form of the latter's buildings has been regulated by varying kinds of government legislation. In London, after the Great Fire had devastated much of the city, the Rebuilding (of London) Act of 1667 imposed an overall height limit on all buildings, depending on the width of the street. Together with building regulations requiring every party wall to be constructed of brickwork, this was to help prevent such a disaster occurring again – as the further the buildings were apart, the less likely it was that a fire could spread. The idea of controlling building heights goes back to ancient Rome where, after a fire in 64 CE, the height of tenement blocks was limited to 70 feet (21 metres).

The height of a building was not the only thing to be controlled. In New York, the degree of daylight that could reach the streets and the lower parts of tall buildings was controlled by a zoning ordinance of 1916, introduced by the city authorities. This resulted in a series of setbacks, or the ziggurat outline that makes New York's early skyscrapers so distinctive in shape. Most conurbations have introduced building regulations at some time, to control the form of new building. In Britain the 1875 Housing Act was a response to the Public Health Act, which laid down minimum hygiene requirements. This was at a time when the benefits of light, air and space in preventing the spread of diseases like cholera and typhus were finally beginning to be recognized. This law stipulated that walls had to be a certain thickness and damp-proofed, and that proper sewage disposal and drainage should be provided. It also meant that for the first time each house had to have its own WC, in addition to water laid on to a sink inside the house and a copper for washing clothes. The regulations specified minimum widths for houses, although these were quite narrow frontages of between 14 and 17 feet (4 and 5 metres) wide. This resulted in houses having narrow street-fronts but deep backs. Since the nineteenth century, zoning, which aims to separate out the various uses of the city, has been a key part of planning legislation. It has been used to separate residential and industrial areas, which are seen as best kept separate, based on lessons learnt from nineteenth-century industrial towns. But local planning regulations and zoning can have disadvantages, by creating antiseptic mono-functional areas, which lack the rich textures that older centres provide.

4.18 Sketch of 'The Business Center'. Hugh Ferriss. A finished version was published in *Metropolis of Tomorrow*, 1929.

Ferriss was one of America's leading architectural illustrators in the 1920s and 1930s. He drew real buildings as well as fantastic creations. Pencil on tracing paper.

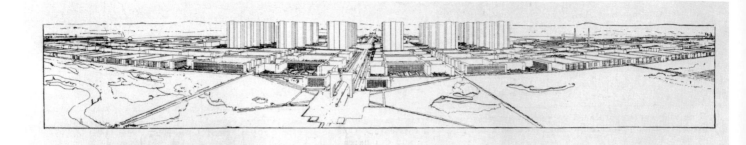

Many critics today attack the town planning theories of the Modern Movement for creating sterile and inhuman environments. But this was not their intention. One of the most radical early schemes that influenced twentieth-century urbanism was devised by Le Corbusier. His 'A Contemporary City of Three Million People', shown at the Salon d'Automne in Paris in 1922 was published in English as 'The City of Tomorrow and its Planning' in 1929. This scheme was zoned in order to avoid congestion in the city centre. The central district contained business and residential areas, whilst a garden city was placed on the periphery with a protected zone (or 'green belt') between the two. The scheme featured 24 skyscrapers, containing apartments and office accommodation, placed some distance apart, with plenty of public open spaces. Significantly, Le Corbusier intended the tower blocks for those who worked and lived in the city, whilst suburban dwellers who worked in the outer industrial zone and did not have to come into the city lived in low-rise garden cities outside.

The project also featured an elaborate road system for cars. Indeed, road users were divided into three main types of traffic: heavy goods, lighter goods and fast traffic. 'Superimposed storeys' of roads were proposed for each type. One of the main ideas was to separate cars from people, in order to decongest the centres of cities. It was later realized that this only works if public transport is adequate. Le Corbusier's ideas were not realized physically until cities like Brasilia, the new capital city of Brazil, and Chandigarh in India were built, with their emphasis on tall buildings in the central district and the dominance of the motor car.

The idea of building high-density blocks within parkland was put into practice in Marseilles with the Unité d'Habitation, designed by Le Corbusier and completed in 1952. This was one of a series of self-contained blocks of flats that provided 'streets in the air', a street of shops in the middle in the building, with access to the flats by 'street decks'. The block was raised up off the ground on columns, called *pilotis*, so that the space underneath could be utilized. Additional amenities for residents were placed on the roof, including a children's playground and swimming pool. Park Hill, in Sheffield, was one of the first British post-war schemes based on this idea and was built 1957–60. Here, four long high-density blocks are linked down a sloping site, with continuous, open access decks every three levels. The decks were meant to imitate the traditional street, although safer to use, with covered spaces for children to play and even enough width for milk floats and other delivery vehicles.

Some town plans, such as Frank Lloyd Wright's unrealized Broadacre City – shown to the public in 1935 – were low-lying and spread out, and featured

4.21 Model of Broadacre City, 1935. Frank Lloyd Wright.

hardly any tall towers. Wright designed for much lower densities than Le Corbusier and created a sprawling plan, in which every person would farm their own acre of land as well as doing factory piecework in their own workshop. The main difference between Wright's plan and that of most Modern Movement architects was that his was based on decentralized policies, requiring little input from government. Usonia in New York State, although not a planned community, was based on these ideas. Its plan is significant because it prefigured the development of many Midwest towns in the USA, with their low density, low-lying nature – and total dependence on the car.

The Radburn system of planning – first applied to the design of Radburn, New Jersey, USA, in the 1920s – included a planning device for keeping traffic and pedestrians separate. This concept was subsequently used in the planning of many towns throughout the world. It encouraged the idea of providing a neighbourhood park between buildings and placing cars in open courts at the back of housing, giving pedestrians access to front doors via footpaths. However, it could confuse the first-time visitor, as whether you approached the front or back of the house depended on whether you had arrived by car or on foot. Some large housing estates, such as the Barbican estate in London, took this idea to the extreme. Here the flats are only accessible on foot from a multi-level sequence of long and confusing open decks, staircases and lifts; cars are left underground. Recently, brightly coloured lines have had to be drawn on the decks for visitors to follow, to find their way around the estate.

4.22 Aerial view of the Las Vegas strip, 1977.

4.23 *A Design Guide for Residential Areas*, front cover. Published by Essex County Council, 1973.

Many of the ideas of the 1920s and 1930s Modern Movement were put into practice in Britain after the Second World War, not only in architectural style but in the form of planning controls. In Britain a huge rebuilding programme was begun; the Labour government was committed to the state provision of decent housing as one of the key elements in the Welfare State programme. This political ideology, combined with Modern Movement ideas, convinced many architects, planners and politicians that good housing would create good citizens, that architecture could determine the way people lived and thought.

Following the perceived failures in much public housing of the immediate post-war period, the concept of using architecture as a form of social control was heavily criticized for being too deterministic. In the USA, Jane Jacob's classic book *The Death and Life of Great American Cities* (1961) showed how the overplanning of our cities, and speculative capital, had made them inhuman places to live. She argued that planning had become too scientific, and that human beings – who are not always rational creatures – cannot be told to live in a certain way. Later a number of critics put forward the notion of 'non-plan': seeing what might happen if places just evolved and were not planned in any way. These ideas partly developed from studies by Reyner Banham and others, on aspects of American culture that they thought would come to influence the European scene. Books such as *Learning from Las Vegas* (1972) by Robert Venturi, Denise Scott-Brown and Steven Izenour, a study of the commercial strip in an unplanned city, also put forward the idea that architects and planners did not have to change the existing environment (as this method did not allow ordinary people to express their own tastes and values), but could enhance what was already there.

Jacobs and others were especially critical of notions of urban planning derived from Modern Movement theory. They were sceptical of planners' theories, for instance of 'neighbourhood units', 'mixed development', 'ideal densities' and other such concepts.

In some parts of the world, not only the size and density of buildings was laid down, but also the look of them. This is not as bizarre as might first be thought. Sumptuary laws that attempted to control not only what people could wear but also excess ornamentation of their homes, had existed in Italy in the fourteenth century, mainly as a way of ensuring that people did not live above their station. In England, the *Essex Design Guide*, first published in 1973 by Essex County Council, tried to control architectural design by recommending a regional vernacular style for new buildings. It aimed not to stifle modern forms or variation, but wanted to achieve a 'better standard of ordinariness'. Design features like steep roof pitches and stained boarding were recommended, and later editions even noted preferred planting species. More recently, at Seaside in Florida (seen in the 1999 film, *The Truman Show*), guidelines for architects were produced that cover not only aspects such as desirable features, specific materials, size and scale of houses, but also siting. This code and others like it are designed to ensure stylistic harmony of the overall development. But to many, it has created a pastel-coloured, highly manicured environment. This so-called 'harmony' easily slips into repetition and monotony – a tendency for the whole environment to look the same.

Economics and land values

The way cities look is always based in part on the economic and political systems controlling them. In capitalist societies, public and private ownership of land co-exist, although planning controls, and the effect they have on property and land, change according to which political group is in power. In many Third World cities there is a severe imbalance between public and private ownership, and subsequent planning controls, which leads to increased squatting. In some South American cities, over a third of the population may be defined as squatters.

Land speculation has been responsible for much new building, often criticized for its low architectural standards because quick financial return is the key motive. Developers have profited considerably, by buying up cheap land and erecting buildings on it. These might then stand empty for several years until the right economic conditions prevail for them to be sold off, or rented at vastly increased profit. This has led to some new buildings remaining empty for years.

Developers have not only transformed parts of our cities, but have built whole self-contained communities. In the USA, the developers Levitt & Sons built three new towns, each called Levittown, during the 1940s and 1950s – first on Long Island, New York; then in New Jersey; and finally in Pennsylvania. These consisted of low-cost homes intended for soldiers returning from the world war. They enabled people to own a house with land around it, part of the American dream. Criticized by the architectural establishment at the time for their suburban character and uniform street patterns, they were liked by their inhabitants (known as 'Levittowners') and the houses sold quickly. The incomers appreciated the semi-rural quality of the place, its safe streets, its privacy and lack of pollution. In Britain in the post-war period, many similar new towns were built, following the New Towns Act of 1946. These were established to ease inner-city congestion by rehousing urban slum-dwellers. People were moved out of Victorian slums in the East End of London into brand new homes with modern amenities like bathrooms and kitchens, as at Harlow in Hertfordshire, one of the first New Towns built in the late 1940s. However, existing neighbourhoods and communities were broken up this way, leaving many people feeling lonely and isolated. This phenomenon became known at the time as the 'New Town blues'. What planners and architects seemed to neglect was that the overall social environment is as important to people as individual homes. This acts, as the architectural critic Christopher Alexander has stated, 'as a mechanism for sustaining human contact'.

Infrastructure

Various planning schemes have sought to provide good transport links to enable the city to function efficiently. In many places, speculative development of the overground and underground railway systems provided the infrastructure for future expansion. Suburbs were developed this way: to house people who would commute to work by rail, making a profit for shareholders. The railway also changed the appearance of cities – sometimes in a detrimental way by the building of high-rise tracks above the roof-line, changing and even obstructing views of some well-known buildings. The building of railway stations has also changed the feel of city districts, by encouraging the provision of hotels, guest houses and other facilities for the traveller. On the other hand, the railway also helped to rejuvenate certain areas or encouraged places to become tourist destinations in their own right, and to develop their cultural attractions.

In many places, cars have transformed the look of cities and how we use them. They have sometimes undermined the city centre and its public spaces, and disadvantaged pedestrians. In Britain in the post-war period, many historic city centres were sliced through by vast road systems, not only creating artificially separate areas, but also disrupting the way people identified with a city. Los Angeles would not have developed in the way it has without the dominance of freeway culture, which has encouraged commuting by car through a vast suburban sprawl. Indeed, in the case of Los Angeles, car manufacturers bought the railways and removed the tracks, so people were forced to use private cars. It is a place that deters pedestrians, who are few and far between, making the city seem under-populated.

Landmark buildings

Many cities have landmark buildings that provide a unique 'sense of place'. For example, Paris would not be Paris without its Eiffel Tower (originally a temporary monument), nor would Sydney be the same without its Opera House. These buildings have become civic symbols. St. Paul's Cathedral, for instance, became a symbol of rebuilt London after the Great Fire, and later epitomized Britain's steadfastness during the Blitz. Generic monuments, such as triumphal arches, are now found in almost every city of the world, used to denote power and civic pride. Some are erected to commemorate an individual or event, or are symbolic of the might of the army. In the nineteenth century, cities like Paris and London erected Egyptian obelisks, following Napoleon's abortive military adventures in North Africa and the fashion for all things Egyptian. The idea was based on the Roman example of erecting obelisks brought back from their occupation of that area.

4.24 London Bridge, Lake Havasu, Arizona, USA. John Rennie.

Originally built 1834, and re-erected on Lake Havasu in 1971.

Sometimes new icon buildings have put hitherto unknown places on the cultural map, as the Guggenheim Museum in Bilbao has done, giving a post-industrial city new life. Some cities have searched for an image, and even used landmark buildings moved from another country to put them on the map. In 1962, Robert McCulloch, a developer who had established the new town of Lake Havasu in Arizona, purchased London Bridge from the British government. He may have believed he was buying the world-famous Tower Bridge, an important London landmark. The early nineteenth-century stone bridge was reconstructed over Lake Havasu, which was establishing itself as a holiday resort. Its connotations with the 'Old World' were not lost, and a plethora of 'Olde Englyshe' shops and red telephone boxes erected nearby have given the city a theme which it uses to market itself.

Not only individual buildings and monuments, but also whole districts can contribute to a city's identity. With the gradual eradication of slums in the West in the twentieth century, many inner cities previously only used during the daytime by office workers (who prefer to live in the suburbs) have been rejuvenated. Previous industrial areas, such as docks or factory sites, have witnessed the reuse of redundant buildings, converted into offices or homes. As districts are gentrified by private developers or turned into conservation areas by local authorities, their physical and cultural make-up changes. They can push the remaining indigenous population out, since they can no longer afford the rising rents. On Manhattan Island, districts once full of warehouses and light industry have been transformed into newly fashionable enclaves. As the old buildings are turned into 'lofts', shops, restaurants and bars, districts have been cleverly marketed with new names like SoHo, Tribeca and NoLita. Many cities have followed this model of sprucing up old quarters. They are turned into marketable commodities for the tourist industry, as well as providing new types of accommodation for the residential community. This has been done by preserving or recreating historical features (cobbled streets, ironwork), and perhaps by the addition of 'retro' street furniture and lighting.

Open-air museums that show how people used to live, or how things used to be made, were first created over a century ago (Skansen in Stockholm opened in the 1890s), but in the late twentieth century they made a comeback in popularity. In Britain in the 1980s many of these museums, like Beamish in County Durham, were created to show visitors a lost way of life. Redundant buildings were moved to the site from a wide area, and recreated to form an idyllic village. Industrial sites too, such as railway villages or ex-colliery towns, have been turned into visitor attractions as part of the booming leisure 'industry'. Here, buildings are reused as a form of historic interpretation: to remind people not only of a lost way of life, but of a lost built environment.

4.25 Beamish Open-air Museum, County Durham, England.

Opened in 1970, this open-air museum recreates life in the north of England at two particular times – the early 19th century and the early 20th century.

TRAFALGAR SQUARE – CREATING THE NATION'S SQUARE

Gareth Williams

London's Trafalgar Square is one of the world's most famous urban spaces. Symbolically it is Britain's heart, as it is from here that all distances to London are measured. Visually it represents 'Britishness' in the common consciousness. Yet it was not built as a single entity, but grew over time from the urban fabric of London. How did Trafalgar Square develop, and why?

The site was between the old City of London and the Palace of Westminster, home to the monarch and the government, and as such became a popular public meeting place. This was where the people petitioned their rulers, and where celebrations or protests were enacted.

The King's stables had been outside the gates of Westminster since the fourteenth century, and in 1732 William Kent improved the site for George II with a large new Royal Mews, a muscular classical building roughly where the National Gallery now stands. The mews was a rare open space in the city's unplanned urban sprawl.

In 1812, the Regency architect John Nash devised a master-plan to improve central

London. For the first time the site was considered as a designed public space. Nash recognized this as where 'the greatest part of the population of the Metropolis meet and diverge', and that 'it could afford a magnificent and beautiful termination of the street from Westminster'.

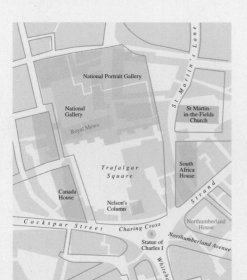

4.26 (left) The present-day plan of Trafalgar Square superimposed on the plan of 1747.

4.27 (above) *The new opening to St Martin's Church from Pall Mall East*, about 1827. H W Bond after Thomas Hosmer Shepherd.

William Kent's Royal Mews stands to the left, opposite the new Royal College of Physicians recently completed by Robert Smirke. In the distance, the older buildings beside St Martin-in-the-Fields would soon be demolished. Engraving. V&A: E 909–2003.

Work on the square dates from the 1820s to the 1840s. By 1827 Pall Mall had been extended east in front of Kent's Royal Mews to join St Martin's Lane, for the first time opening up a direct view of the portico of St Martin-in-the-Fields (1722–6) by James Gibbs, the oldest building in the present-day square. This street defined the square's northern edge. The lower stretch of St Martin's Lane was demolished in the 1820s to make way for Morley's Hotel on the square's eastern side. The first grand civic building of Nash's master-plan was Robert Smirke's College of Physicians (1824–7, later modified as Canada House), marking the west of the site.

A new national gallery was proposed to dominate the elevated north side of the square in place of the mews. William Wilkins's rather low and incoherently detailed National Gallery (1834–8) lacks presence for such an elevated and prestigious site, especially as Charles Barry isolated it on a raised terrace in the 1840s.

The site was christened Trafalgar Square in 1830, in honour of Lord Nelson's decisive naval victory over the Napoleonic fleet in 1805.

4.28 (below) *Trafalgar Square, the National Gallery, St Martin's Church*, 1852. T Picken after E Walker.

All the components of the modern square are in place. By 1867 Sir Edwin Landseer had replaced the recumbent lions shown at the foot of Nelson's Column with altogether more regal beasts. Coloured lithograph. V&A: E 911–2003.

4.29 (bottom) Redevelopment of Trafalgar Square, 2003. Foster and Partners with Atkins Landscape Consultants.

Traffic has been removed from the north side of the square, reconnecting the National Gallery and the square with a new monumental stair.

A select committee in 1840 worried about the Nelson monument's scale, noting that 'it is desirable in a great city to suggest the idea of space, and having obtained space, not to block it up again'. Perhaps the politicians were right. The vast Corinthian column, completed in 1843 by William Railton, overwhelms all the surrounding buildings.

Nelson's Column established Trafalgar Square as a site of imperial and military public commemoration and it now hosts monuments to numerous worthies. By 1852 the square was completed, including fountains and pools inserted in 1845 to make it less convenient for public insurrections and riots.

Few changes have dramatically affected Trafalgar Square since. Morley's Hotel gave way to Sir Herbert Baker's spare, neo-classical South Africa House by 1935, completing the eastern flank. Together with Admiralty Arch (1911 by Sir Aston Webb) and Canada House opposite, British imperial might was underscored.

By the twentieth century the square was the site of national celebration – for example New Year's Eve and V E Day – for political debate and dissent, and even of anarchy – such as the 1990 Poll Tax Riot. The last major building was an addition to the National Gallery opened in 1991, designed by Venturi, Scott Brown and Associates. It deconstructs the classical orders of the square's other buildings across the width of its façade.

By then, traffic congestion and Trafalgar Square's axial position in the city had virtually reduced it to a roundabout island. Foster and Partners' redevelopment, of 2003, closed the north side to traffic, creating a new public plaza and monumental stair connecting the National Gallery to the square before it. The scheme re-emphasizes public ownership of the site by enhancing access to it and confirming its role as the nation's square.

Human impact

All of us live and work in buildings, and use the spaces around them; they affect our lives every day. We are often not aware of their effect unless they touch us in a negative way (there is too much glass and sunshine makes the building too hot, or the air-conditioning makes us feel ill), or have emotional qualities (the feelings we might experience in a cathedral interior, or when looking at a mausoleum in a cemetery or even visiting Disneyland). In some cultures, people participate directly in building their own homes, or actively shape their immediate environment by getting involved. Large developments such as housing estates and city centre schemes have a direct effect on people's lives, particularly their sense of community and identity. Some people enjoy the sense of anonymity they feel in a crowded busy city, whilst others prefer the sense of a closeness in a small agricultural settlement, away from all crowds. Architects and planners have tried, with varying degrees of success, to plan how buildings and urban spaces will be used by the people who occupy them. When this does not work, it can be an unmitigated disaster – causing alienation.

Two types of building which affect people every day are their homes and the shops they visit. Homes give people a sense of belonging and security, and we all like to project our identity on to them. We can often make our personal spaces unique by customizing what we have, for instance by adding stone cladding to the outside of our home, or by tending flower boxes on window sills, or by simply decorating the inside. In the West, where the majority of us live in a mass consumer society, it has become even more important to mark our individuality. When we do not have the freedom to adapt our homes, or we dislike the uniformity of our surroundings, we might respond by various means of protest: by graffiti or vandalism, even – in extreme cases – by suicide. Public housing estates have been especially criticized for their lack of definition between public and private space. On the whole, people do not feel responsibility for shared spaces like lifts, staircases or communal gardens. These areas are considered the responsibility of the 'other': the local council, who may, or may not, have sufficient resources to keep them maintained. The concept of 'defensible space', first identified in 1972, is the theory that everyone needs the space immediately outside their own home, to call their own.

Many housing estates built in the post-war period, intended to provide affordable and rational accommodation, have since been demolished. The key example, Pruitt-Igoe in St Louis, Missouri, built in the late 1950s was, by the late 1960s, abandoned and later blown up. But other similar types of housing have survived, and some have even made a successful comeback. Trellick Tower, part of the Edenham Street estate in North Kensington, designed by Ernö Goldfinger for the Greater London Council in the late 1960s, was intended by the architect to provide utopian living. Initially successful, it quickly fell from grace. At one time during its life span it was considered part of a 'sink estate'. This was not improved by the council's policy of putting young families, and later refugees, into the flats. The flats, however, were well designed, detailed and planned, some with large south-west-facing balconies and good views, double-height living rooms and communal facilities on the roof. These kinds of features kept a significant proportion of the residents living and raising their children in them for decades. They also felt empowered to establish a residents' association, in order to confront the council collectively for certain issues. The block was restored in the 1990s, with video entryphones installed and a porter on the front desk. Some flats were sold off to

4.30 Design for Trellick Tower, Edenham Street estate, North Kensington, London, 1967. Ernö Goldfinger.

Drawing by John Bains.
Pen on tracing paper.
RIBA Library Drawings Collection.

4.31 Shopping precinct, Coventry, Warwickshire, England, 1957. Coventry Architects Department.

RIBA Library Photographs Collection/John McCann.

private owners. The estate's physical context, in an area of Victorian working-class housing but adjacent to a now gentrified Notting Hill, contributed to its revival. In the 1990s, tower blocks generally (and Goldfinger's certainly) were reappraised. Trellick Tower was subsequently listed by English Heritage, ensuring that it is maintained and that little can be altered without permission. It perhaps demonstrates the idea that good social housing is not just reliant on quality or the architectural style of the estate, but also on social factors.

In the West, many local authorities have renewed their housing stock, particularly that built in the post-war boom. This sometimes involves repair, or demolition and rebuilding, or diversification of tenure. In some instances, the image of the housing has been updated. For instance, some tower blocks have been externally remodelled with the addition of brightly coloured pitched roofs, balconies and entrance canopies, in an effort to make them 'consumer-friendly' and individual. Although its effect is often unquantifiable, this element of housing renewal, together with improved security and other social factors, makes a difference to people's surroundings and can give them pride in where they live.

Another day-to-day activity that has changed over time, and affected people's lives considerably, is shopping. In the post-war period, shopping centres developed from earlier street markets, arcades and gallerias into open-air pedestrian precincts. One of the first of this kind in Britain was at Coventry, built in the early 1950s, which exploited its sloping site to provide two levels of shops, inspired by the rows of Chester: a sixteenth-century street of multi-level shops. In Britain, the first pedestrianized shopping centres, open-air or enclosed, were always situated in the middles of cities rather than on the peripheries. Some were built as part of a wider reconstruction programme to replace bombed centres. Others were built due to the availability of land, and the lack of private transport required to travel to outlying shopping centres – unlike the situation in the United States.

In many Western countries in the post-war period, planning incentives and the profit motive increasingly led to the growth of out-of-town shopping centres, generally on the North American pattern. This was usually at the cost of traditional high street shops, which lost out as their customers were drawn out of town. Sometimes large multiples killed off locally owned shops by undercutting prices, and led to deserted city centres. The growth of shopping malls and mass car ownership (and associated car parks) also reflected new marketing methods, particularly the idea of bulk buying and one-stop shopping. Malls are part of the boom in the leisure industry, in which consumption – 'retail therapy' – has become a new kind of recreation.

Out-of-town shopping centres have been criticized for ignoring those members of society who are unable to use them, the elderly, disabled or the very young, or those without private transport. Many cater for a specifically middle-class market. Others are designed to offer a variety of shopping experiences for different kinds of people. At the Bluewater development in Kent, opened in 1999 and built in a disused chalk quarry, three kinds of shopping experiences are provided in addition to an entertainment centre. The development is based on a triangular plan, 'anchored' on each corner by a major multiple store and by three 'villages'. The architect, Eric Kuhne, has tried to counteract the usual blandness and monotony of shopping mall design by introducing colour, decoration and sculpture to bring

4.32 Bluewater shopping centre, Kent, England, 1998–9. Eric Kuhne Architects.

a sense of uniqueness to the centre, as well as to socially stratify different areas. Regionalism is evident in the form of murals and bas-reliefs that evoke local rural culture, myths and legends. In a sense, the architect combined the concept of the big shopping development with the intimacy of local shopping. Like Bluewater, many centres also play a leading role in the local community by hosting cultural events, such as concerts.

The shopping mall is said to have been born in the USA. Architecturally, its main distinction is that the shops usually face inwards, towards each other, so that visitors first see the backs of the shops (and perhaps their loading bays) from the car park that surrounds them, rather than the fronts of the shops. Malls are marketed as providing a happy, family-oriented experience. For many without financial means though, they can be soul-destroying. Their clinical, sanitized environments, controlled by security guards and surveillance cameras, can bring feelings of alienation and vulnerability.

How people can affect their built environment: self-help

Many people who feel powerless against the authorities have devised other means of getting the homes they want, and of building new kinds of communities. One instance of this phenomenon was 'plotlands', developed in various sites in England in the 1920s and 1930s before strict planning controls were brought in. These were areas of speculatively built, cheap homes intended as holiday or weekend places, but usually lacking basic services. Local councils tried unsuccessfully to remove the houses and residents by retrospective legislation. The residents enjoyed the feeling of community and the freedom of customizing their homes in the way they liked, without being told what they could and could not do. In many northern European countries, the allotment-garden tradition has continued on the outskirts of urban centres, with basic sheds erected on them for people to visit and tend at weekends, and with fewer planning controls than in purely residential districts.

In countries that provide little social welfare, the poorest people, often migrant workers who would otherwise be homeless, have no choice but to live in slum social housing – or to act collectively by appropriating certain areas through squatting. Unable to earn enough to pay high rents, and with no extended family nearby to offer support, the migrants transform districts into ghettos or *barrios*, such as in Lima, Peru, where over a quarter of the population lives this way. Acting collectively and using professionals, squatters can earmark some government-owned land and then invade it overnight, chalking out the housing plots and erecting simple shacks over a matter of days. These are replaced later by more permanent buildings of bricks and mortar, or extended with additional storeys, as or when needs be. As the camp becomes established and grows, the squatters form their own organizations, hold elections and may be able to pressurize the authorities into providing essential services such as running water and sewerage.

4.33 Jaywick Sands, Clacton, Essex, England, built from 1928.

One of the 'plotlands' developments of the inter-war period.

Alternative architecture

The realization that many planning theories advocated by the Modern Movement were failing the very people they were meant to assist led to the idea of direct participation in the 1960s. This developed into two strands. On the one hand, the idea emerged of people-built, non-architect-designed buildings, as a manifestation of hippy culture. The other strand consisted of architect-designed, futuristic projects that offered alternative ways of living. In the West, the 'land of plenty', the counter-culture phenomenon led to the establishment of many alternative communities, particularly in the south-western United States, built by those who lived in them. Drop City, founded on the outskirts of Trinidad, Colorado, by architectural students c.1967, was the first hippy dome community – a kind of building later called 'funk architecture'. Domes were easy to build by hand and from 'found' materials, such as car parts. Other basic forms of shelter, such as tents, were also used in these alternative communities as they could be erected quickly and cheaply. These and similar projects questioned the roles of architect and planner: if people could create their own environment, why did they need architects?

The idea of alternative ways of living grew from utopian town-planning schemes of the nineteenth century and earlier. These were developed by philanthropists or industrialists who sought to improve their workers' lives, or by religious dissenters persecuted by the established Church and seeking alternative ways of living. Robert Owen, a social reformer, founded a cooperative community at New Lanark in Scotland, before moving the settlement to New Harmony, Indiana. Others described completely utopian societies based on an idealized pre-industrial past, such as the design reformer William Morris in *News from Nowhere* (1888).

In the twentieth century, a number of architects formalized their ideas by producing schemes designed for alternative living. These were new kinds of environments for human activity, based on the real or imagined potential of new technologies. Some were on a large scale, others were small-scale, personal environments. Some visionary projects for new cities were more influential for the architectural forms they suggested than for ideas of what a modern city could actually be like. The idea that cities should not have to last long, but could be remade when needed, had been suggested by the Italian Futurist architect Antonio Sant'Elia. His 'Città Nuova', a series of drawings exhibited in 1914, showed a futuristic urban environment, densely packed and geared towards industry. The tall buildings featured exterior elevators, and roads on three levels; he showed separated-out transportation networks – including pedestrian, rail, and car routes – but none of his schemes made any reference to the real parts of a city, to nature or to human scale. Futuristic designs for cities have also appeared in works of popular fiction and science fiction films for over a century. These have both influenced future built environments and taken ideas from contemporary life. *Things to Come* (1936), directed by Alexander Korda, shows a multi-storey metropolis of the twenty-first century, built by scientists and engineers. Modernism is portrayed in the use of smooth, functional glass skyscrapers, whose wide terraces look down on to the public plaza below. Suspended footbridges and lifts in the form of glass cylinders provide a positive view of future civilization, in which architecture represents the machine. Ridley Scott's *Blade Runner* (1982), on the other hand, invents a dystopian Los Angeles of 2019, in which neon lighting and sophisticated technology are juxtaposed against a decaying postmodern world of past architectural styles under constant rain. In a sense, the future is portrayed as the past.

The Italian architect Paolo Soleri planned a number of self-contained and experimental communities from the 1950s, and did much research into urban planning. Still in development, his 'urban laboratory', Arcosanti, is situated north of Phoenix, Arizona. Intended eventually to house 5,000 people, the community is meant to demonstrate ways of improving urban conditions and lessening man's destructive impact on the earth. In construction since 1970, the scheme consists of semi-circular concrete domes used for communal activities such as meetings and concerts, in addition to more conventional three-storey living

4.34 'La Città Nuova', drawing of an apartment building, 1914. Antonio Sant'Elia.

Taken from *L'architettura futurista*. Manifesto, Milan, 11 July 1914. RIBA Library Photographs Collection.

4.35 Arcosanti, near Phoenix, Arizona, built from 1970. Paolo Soleri.

4.36 Design for Plug-in City: University Node, 1965. Archigram. Peter Cook.

This unexecuted design, part of Plug-in City, was an ongoing student project at the Architectural Association, designed to use expendable units. Mixed media on paper. V&A: Circ.254–1973.

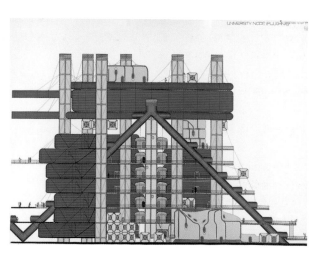

accommodation. These are compactly arranged so as to preserve the natural landscape and to keep it close to the residents. The scheme is designed according to 'arcology', a concept devised by Soleri in which architecture and life interact, with the efficient circulation of people, multi-purpose buildings and the use of solar power.

Often architects' plans for alternative ways of living are simply imaginary, and never really intended to be taken seriously. Archigram, a group of British architects formed in the early 1960s, designed a number of radical 'megastructures'. Although never built, their schemes were published and exhibited by the group, and in many ways were prototypes of the high-tech buildings of the 1970s, such as the Pompidou Centre in Paris. In this building, and others like it, the services are placed on the outside visible to the eye, so creating a striking architectural aesthetic. One of Archigram's schemes, the Plug-in City, consisted of living units that plugged into a service network or structure, resulting in a landscape of uneven towers. Their projects were based on contemporary research into space technologies and pop culture and, above all, summed up the optimism and free-love culture of the period. Their buildings were designed for obsolescence; they believed that cities should be able to adapt and change according to need. They considered too that different kinds of building should have different lifespans, and that some would change more rapidly than others.

Similarly, the Italian architectural practice Superstudio had an idea to build one enormous superstructure, the *Monumento Continuo*, initially over New York City, but eventually covering the entire surface of the planet. This consisted of a smooth-surfaced three-dimensional grid, with gaps through which existing buildings of the old city could protrude. It was their reaction to globalization, in which they saw local cultures and individual expression being subsumed by a global grid. Superstudio was different from Archigram in that they took on board the need to overthrow the existing political and economic system if such schemes were ever to get built. Archigram, on the other hand, assumed a society where mobility was free, but ignored the political aspect of who produced or controlled the system.

Real public participation

Much of the criticism of planning legislation is due to people feeling excluded from the design process, frustrated that they are unable to determine their own environment. Communities have often needed to fight local authorities to get their homes or streets improved. In some cases when people fight collectively, such as on housing estates, improvements are made – but it is usually an uphill struggle. Some effort was made to change this situation in the 1960s, through government legislation. In Britain the Skeffington Report of 1969 gave recommendations to local authorities on how to involve the public in planning decisions, for example in the form of community forums, so that people were able to have a voice. At the same time in the USA, advocacy planning grew from similar legislation that laid down citizen participation. Advocacy planning, which involved a middle person who could represent the needs of the community and communicate these to the local planning authority, had particular success with housing rehabilitation schemes. In the 1970s self-help community architecture developed from this, in which residents – working with architects – developed their ideas for how their new housing might look and work, using basic paper and models in a very hands-on and instant way. Often, the residents had the initial ideas, but needed the architect to translate them into a final design.

One classic instance of public participation, involving inhabitants determining the form of their new housing, was the Byker estate in Newcastle, begun in the late 1960s. The project involved the resettlement of an established community who lived in terraced Victorian houses initially built for shipyard workers. The majority of the population, when canvassed, were all for redevelopment of their housing, but still wanted to retain the atmosphere of their existing community and keep their social ties. The architect of the scheme, Ralph Erskine, stayed at Byker for a month, set up an office and collaborated with the local people, listening to their hopes and fears for the new estate. When asked, tenants wanted modern features like open-plan rooms and bright colours, but wanted to keep certain old features like corner shops and pubs. The architects took much of this on board, making an effort to retain the area's character in terms of its atmosphere, site and people. Although the scheme was seen as successful, it has been criticized for raising expectations that could not be fulfilled. But development there has not stopped. More recently, residents' pressure was responsible for a change in location of the car-parking areas, now introduced conveniently outside their homes, rather than some distance away (*see plate 4.37*).

Architects have turned to new ways of involving the public in the building and design process. The Segal method of self-build, devised by the architect Walter Segal in the 1960s (initially for himself and his family), allows people with no previous experience to build their own homes, determining both their look and function, using simple construction techniques and sustainable materials. Using a timber frame, buildings can also be adapted as needed. But because these types of houses are individually built they have faced

**4.37 The Byker Wall,
Byker Housing Development,
Newcastle-upon-Tyne,
England, 1969–80.
Ralph Erskine.**

RIBA Library Photographs
Collection/Daniel George
Kantorowich.

some hostility, particularly from planning authorities and with obtaining finance for the project.

This chapter has endeavoured to show that the built environment always reflects the attitudes and sensibilities of the time and the place. Buildings grouped together, whether in towns or cities, are the practical response to the aspirations of the people that helped to create them. This includes both the users and designers. Current thinking centres on how to make our cities environmentally sustainable, so as not to waste the world's depleting resources. As cities seem to be increasingly consuming the countryside, the idea of creating so-called 'eco villages' and 'eco cities' has been promoted since the end of twentieth century (although a sustainable city is possibly a contradiction in terms). This idea may soon not be a choice, but mandatory. Some countries like the USA use more power than others. But cities like Los Angeles, in the 'Sunshine State', choose not to use its natural climate (the sun) for electrical power. Relying on air-conditioning for comfort, the resulting pressure on power supply causes 'brown-outs' (short-term decreases in voltage levels).

To be successful, towns and cities have to work for a multitude of users, and provide a variety of functions. If they do not, chaos and social upheaval may occur. This can result in the establishment of two separate communities, suburban enclaves and inner-city slums. Mike Davis, a lecturer in urban theory in southern California, has reflected on how the redevelopment of Los Angeles has resulted in just such a separation in his book *City of Quartz: Excavating the Future in Los Angeles* (1990). He describes how the city's authorities tried to zone certain parts of the city, in order to keep them single-class and single-ethnicity. To keep 'undesirables' – the poor – out of rich white middle-class areas, the authorities used a number of methods, including new freeways and street barriers that cut through existing street patterns. The passive-aggressive dark glass façades of corporate office buildings, and the security patrols in shopping malls, also helped to kill off the concept of the street. Davis particularly laments how downtown Los Angeles has become an enclave for the poorest of society, the Latinos and blacks, and how no foresight has been given to creating an inclusive city.

Many critics argue that cities have become over-designed and over-determined. Time, and how cities might be allowed to evolve, is usually not considered by planners. Add to this the short life span of most modern buildings, and it is clear that no one plans or builds for longer than their own lifetime. Short-sighted political systems control these initiatives. Architecture and town planning are continually working within these constraints, reacting to financial or sociological change outside their control. It is usually not the fault of one particular side when things go wrong. Towns and cities, where buildings are closest together, are like living organisms. With different functions and requirements they live, die and are constantly regenerated.

PICTURE CREDITS

All illustrations are copyright RIBA or V&A Museum except for the following:

Alinari Picture Library: 1.36, 2.39, 3.15, 3.20, 4.5, 4.12
Arcaid: 1.44, 1.48, 2.60, 3.23
Arcosanti, Ken Howie: 4.35

Bastin & Evrard 3.36 (© Dacs 2004)
Bauhaus-Archiv Museum of Design, Berlin: 2.58
Beamish Open Air Museum: 4.25
Professor T. J. Benton: 3.34
Berlin Picture Service: 4.10
Bibliothèque Nationale de France, Paris: 2.46
Bildarchiv Foto Marburg: 3.9
bounford.com 4.26
City of Bristol Museum: 4.4
British Library: 1.7

Commission on Chicago Landmarks: 3.37
Keith Collie: 2.57
Columbia University: 4.18
Concrete Information: 3.32
Corbis: Intro.1, Intro.9, 1.2, 1.23, 1.24, 1.39, 2.11, 2.14, 2.18, 2.28, 2.36, 3.2, 3.12 (©ARS, NY and DACS, London 2004), 3.18, 3.19, 3.29, 4.24
Le Corbusier 2.1, 2.59, 3.44, 4.20 (© FLC/ADAGP, Paris and DACS, London, 2004)

Walter Denny: 1.37
Frank den Oudsten: 1.33 (© DACS 2004)
Digital Archive of American Architecture, Professor Jeffery Howe: 2.33, 2.50 (©ARS, NY and DACS, London 2004)

Essex County Council: 4.23
Esto, © Ezra Stoller: 4.16

Michael Freeman: 2.51
Foster & Partners: front jacket, 1.3, 1.14, 3.10, 3.39, 4.29
Foto Vasari Archivio: 2.41
Fundaçao Oscar Niemeyer: 1.20

Getty Images: Intro.8, 2.12, 2.30, 2.31
Glasgow School of Art: School of Architecture, Dr Robert Proctor 1.49
Professor Thom Gorst: 4.33
Len Grant: Intro.2
Martin Gray: 3.27
Grove Art Dictionary 2.22
Solomon R. Guggenheim Foundation: frontispiece

Hiroyuki Hirai: 3.11

Irish Heritage Service: 1.25
Yasuhiro Ishimoto: 2.23, 2.24

Matthew Jalbert: 3.31
Jewish Museum Berlin, photo Jens Ziehe: Intro.11

S. C. Johnson Inc: 1.43 (© ARS, NY and DACS, London 2004)

A. F. Kersting: Intro.7, 2.40, 2.42, 2.45, 3.5, 4.2
KLCC (Holdings) BHD: 1.8
Eric Kuhne Architects: 4.32

Landesbildstelle, Berlin: 2.13
Collection David Lawrence: 4.22
Norman Lucey: 4.17

Barbara McKenzie: 2.56
Magnum Photographic: 4.6
Merseyside Photo Library, Ron Jones: 1.35
Christopher Middleton: 2.37

National Gallery of Art, Washington: 2.26
National Monuments Record: Intro.6
National Trust Photographic Library: 1.27, 1.28
New York Public Library: 4.15

Centre Pompidou (by kind permission of Les Amis de la Maison de Verre): 3.40
Clovis Prevost: 3.8

Radha-raman das and Pavan-suta das: 2.20
Bharath Ramamrutham: 2.54
Rex Features: 2.34
The Ritz Hotel: 2.3
Royal Geographical Society 4.9

Collection of Moshe Safdie and Associates, Timothy Hurlsey: 3.25
Smithson Family Collection 3.42
Smithsonian Photographic Services: 4.3
Commercial postcard, collection of Michael Snodin: 3.4
Soane Museum: Intro.13
Stiftelsen Skansen, Marie Andersson: 1.26
stockphotography.co.uk: 2.48
Studio E Architects: 1.16, 1.17

Technical Art Services: 1.38, 2.9
Libor Teply: 1.12
Thames & Hudson: 1.34
Trinity College, Manuscripts Department, Dublin: 3.45

Herman van Doorn, for Zwarts & Jansma Architects: Intro.10
View Pictures: 1.15, 1.18, 1.19

Derek Walker Associates: 4.7
Weald & Downland Openair Museum: 3.43
Christopher Wilson: 3.17
Frank Lloyd Wright Foundation: 4.21 (© ARS, NY and DACS, London , 2004)

Ken Yeang: 1.10

NOTES ON CONTRIBUTORS

Neil Bingham is an architectural historian and design commentator. He was previously Assistant Curator of the Drawings Collection, British Architectural Library, Royal Institute of British Architects. His last book, with Andrew Weaving, was *Modern Retro: Living with Mid-Century Modern Style*.

Charles Hind is H. J. Heinz Curator of Drawings and Assistant Director (Special Collections) at the RIBA Library. He is an architectural historian who has worked previously for the British Library, Sotheby's and the Grove *Dictionary of Art*. A Fellow of the Society of Antiquaries, he also leads art tours studying St Petersburg, and Palladio and the Villas of the Veneto.

Tanishka Kachru obtained a BA from the University of Bombay in 1998 and worked as an architect for two years. In 2002, she received an MA (History of European Decorative Arts) from the Parsons School of Design, New York. She worked as curatorial assistant in the Drawings and Prints Department of the Cooper-Hewitt, National Design Museum before joining the V&A as Assistant Curator in the Department of Projects.

David Lloyd Jones is a founding director of Studio E Architects. He is an acknowledged expert and innovator in energy-conscious and sustainable architecture. His projects include the Renewable Energy Centre, the first commercial zero-energy building in the world. His book, *Architecture and the Environment* was published by Laurence King Publishing in 1998 and is available in five languages.

Helen Thomas is Architecture Education Officer for the V&A+RIBA Architecture Partnership. As an architect she has practised in London and Seville, and she has taught at the Architectural Association, the Bartlett and London Metropolitan University.

Gareth Williams is Curator of the Architecture Gallery at the V&A. He has curated many exhibitions at the V&A including 'Ron Arad Before and After Now' (with Sorrel Hershberg, 2000), 'Brand.New' (with Jane Pavitt, 2000), 'Milan in a Van' (2002) and 'Matali Crasset: Unpacking Design' (2003). He has written and contributed to numerous books including *Brand New* (V&A, 2000) and *Branded?* (V&A, 2000).

Rob Wilson is a writer and an architect and the Curator at the RIBA Gallery, Royal Institute of British Architects. He recently curated the exhibition 'Coming Homes: 3.8 million reasons to think about housing' and co-curated 'Fantasy Architecture: 1500–2036', a National Touring Exhibition at the Hayward Gallery.

CHRONOLOGY OF BUILDINGS, TECHNOLOGY AND EVENTS

DATES	BUILDINGS	TECHNOLOGY	EVENTS TIMELINE
BCE			
		Villages built of dry brick with vaulted stone foundations, Mesopotamia, 5000 BCE.	Start of crop cultivation and domestication of animals. First permanent settlements, Near East, c.8000 BCE.
			Start of Egyptian Old Kingdom, 3100 BCE.
	Stepped pyramid, Sakkâra, Egypt, 2778 BCE.	Ashlar first used at stepped pyramid, Sakkâra, Egypt, 2778 BCE.	Start of Sumerian city states, Mesopotamia, c.3000 BCE.
		Corbelled arch used in Egypt or Greece.	Start of Egyptian Middle Kingdom, 2400 BCE.
	Ziggurat, Ur, Iraq, 2100 BCE.	Mud bricks used at stepped pyramid, Ur, 2100 BCE.	Start of Mycenean civilization, Greece, c.1500 BCE.
	Longhouses, Vitlycke Museum, Tanum, Sweden, originally built 2000 BCE.	Round arch in use, 2000 BCE.	Start of Egyptian New Kingdom, 1304 BCE.
	The Hypostyle Hall, Temple of Amun-Ra, Luxor, Thebes, Egypt, c.1312–1301 BCE.		First appearance of Olmec civilization, central America, c.1200 BCE.
			Start of Vedic age in India, c.1000 BCE.
			Growth of Greek city states, c.900 BCE.
roman times			Rome founded 753 BCE, sacked 410 CE.
			Start of Greek colonization of Mediterranean, c.750 BCE.
			Greatest power of Assyrian empire, Middle East, c.700 BCE.
			Buddha born, 563 BCE.
	Temple of Hera, Paestum, Italy, about 530 BCE.		Confucius begins teaching, 531 BCE.
			Start of Roman Republic, 509 BCE.
			Athenian empire at its height: the classical age, c. 470 BCE.
	The Parthenon, Athens, 447–432 BCE.		Maurya, King of Ashoka, first empire in India, 300 BCE.
			China united under Ch'ing Dynasty, 221 BCE.
			Greece conquered by Rome, 146 BCE.
CE			Birth of Christ, 4.
1st and 2nd centuries	The Great Stupa, Sanchi, India, 1st century CE.		Marcus Vitruvius Pollio writes *De Architectura*, 1–25.
	Cones of Cappadocia, Turkey, 1st century CE.		
	Roman aqueduct, Segovia, Spain, 1st and 2nd centuries CE.	Kiln-baked bricks used for most buildings.	Buddhism reaches China, c.50.
	The Colosseum, Rome, 72–82 CE.	Bronze drawing instruments found in ruins of Pompeii, 79 CE.	
	The Pantheon, Rome, 120–4 CE.	Hollow bricks used for arched roofs.	Roman imperial power at its height, 117.
		Underfloor heating in use.	
		Barrel-vaults developed.	
3rd and 4th centuries	Basilica of Constantine or Maxentius, Rome, 306–30 CE.	Concrete used for vaulted or domed structures.	Start of Mayan culture, Central America, c.300.
			Emperor Constantine legalizes Christianity, 312.
			Emperor Constantine moves capital of Roman Empire to Constantinople, 324.
			Hindu civilization at its height, India, c.400.
			Fall of Western Roman Empire, 476.
5th and 6th centuries			Justinian Emperor of Eastern Roman Empire, 527–65.
	Hagia Sophia, Istanbul, Turkey, 532–62 CE.	Pendentive domes developed.	St Benedict devises the rule governing the organization and spread of Monasticism, c.530.
	San Apollinare in Classe, Ravenna, Italy, about 534–49 CE.		
7th and 8th centuries	Serpent-jaw doorway, Chicanná, Mexico, 600–830 CE.		Birth of Mohammed, 570.
	The Dome of the Rock, Jerusalem, Israel, begun 688 CE.		Arab conquest of Egypt.
	The Kailasa temple, Ellora, India, 757–75 CE.		Moors conquer Iberian peninsula, 711.
	The Prayer Hall of the Great Mosque, Cordoba, Spain, about 785 CE.		
9th and 10th centuries			
			Charlemagne, King of Franks, crowned Holy Roman Emperor, 800.
			Start of rise of urban Europe, c.900.
11th century			
	Durham Cathedral, County Durham, England, 1093–1133.		Norman conquest of England, 1066.
12th century	Angkor Wat, Cambodia, 12th century CE.	Oldest Eastern building manual printed, the Chinese 'Yingzao Fashi' (the State Building standards), by Li Chieh, 1103.	First Crusade, 1096.
	Asinelli and Garisenda Towers, Bologna, Italy, 1109–19.	Caen stone imported to Britain from France.	
		Flying buttresses invented, to carry the weight of a building, 1137.	
	Fountains Abbey, Yorkshire, England, begun 1140.	Rib & fan vaulting developed, in which the weight is taken down on columns, not walls.	
	Chartres Cathedral, France, about 1194–1220.		
13th century	The mud mosque of Djénné, Mali, West Africa, 13th or 14th century.		
	Stave Church from Gol, Norwegian Folk Museum, Oslo, Norway, about 1200.		

DATES	BUILDINGS	TECHNOLOGY	EVENTS TIMELINE
	Grand Canal, Venice, Italy, from 13th century.	Clear glass invented in Venice, 1291.	
	Cloth Hall, Ypres, Belgium, 1202–1304.	Skill of brick-making reintroduced to Britain.	
	Reims Cathedral, France, 1211–1481.	Cruck construction in use.	
	Caernarfon Castle, Wales, 1283–1330.	Braced timber framing in use.	
14th century	The Court of Lions, Alhambra, Granada, Spain, 1338–90.	Hammer-beam roofs developed.	
	The cloister, Gloucester Cathedral, Gloucestershire, England, 1351–77.	Tracing floors made of soft plaster used in cathedrals, on which to draw scaled plans or diagrams.	
	Westminster Hall, London, rebuilt 1394–1402.	Craftsmen formed guilds relating to their trade.	
15th century	Dwellings in Taos pueblo, New Mexico, USA, from about 1400.		
	Florence Cathedral, Italy, from 1296. Dome 1420–36.		
	The Foundling Hospital, Florence, Italy, 1421.		
	King's College Chapel, Cambridge, England, about 1441.		
	Medici Palace (Palazzo Riccardi), Florence, Italy, from 1444.		
		Caxton's first printing press, 1476.	Ottoman Turks conquer Constantinople, 1453.
		Introduction of canon.	
		Discovery of perspective.	Moors expelled from Spain. Columbus reaches America, 1492.
		Paper became more readily available but parchment or vellum used until now.	
16th century	The House of Raphael (Palazzo Caprini), Rome, about 1501.		
	The Tempietto, San Pietro in Montorio, Rome, 1502.		
			Start of Reformation, 1517.
			Founding of Jesuit order, 1540.
	The Suleimaniye Mosque, Istanbul, Turkey, 1551–8.		Sebastiano Serlio publishes first illustration of the orders as a set, 1540.
	Little Moreton Hall, Cheshire, England, 1559.		Council of Trent: start of Counter-reformation, 1545.
	The Escorial, Madrid, Spain, 1559–84.		
	Villa Capra (or Rotonda), Vicenza, Italy, 1565–9.	Pencil drawing becomes widespread, 1565.	
		Geometrical fortifications developed.	
			Andrea Palladio publishes the *Four Books of Architecture*, 1570.
	Palma Nuova, Veneto, Italy, 1593–1623.		
17th century	Himeji Castle, Japan, about 1601–9.		Turks defeated at Battle of Lepanto, 1571.
	The Sultanahmet Mosque, Istanbul, Turkey, 1609–16.	Sash window invented in France.	
	Katsura Imperial Villa, Kyoto, Japan, 1615–63.	Wattle & daub used as cladding material up until this time.	
	Taj Mahal, Agra, India, 1630–53.	Flemish-bond brickwork became more popular than English bond.	
	Gate of the Shrine of Ieyasu Tokugawa, first Tokugawa Shogun, Nikko, Japan, 1634–6.	Tile-hanging in Britain developed.	
	San Carlo alle Quattro Fontane, Rome, 1638–77.	Weatherboarding taken to east coast of US by first settlers from Europe.	
	The Scala Regia, The Vatican, Rome, 1663–6.	Royal Society founded, 1660. Wren a founder member.	Louis XIV, King of France, 1643–1715.
	East front of the Palace of the Louvre, Paris, 1667–70.		
	The Chapel of the Holy Shroud, Turin, Italy, 1668–94.		Great Fire of London, 1666.
	The Staircase of the Ambassadors, Palace of Versailles, France, about 1671.		
	St Paul's Cathedral, London, 1675–1711.		
	Charles Fort, County Cork, Ireland, 1678.		
18th century	Blenheim Palace, Oxfordshire, England, 1704–20.	Coke employed in smelting iron, 1709. Meant cast iron could be produced in greater quantities and more cheaply.	
	St Martin-in-the-Fields, London, 1722–6.		
	Chiswick House, London, about 1725.		
	St John Nepomuk, Munich, Germany, 1733–46.		
	The Panthéon (Ste Geneviève), Paris, 1755–92.		
	Kedleston Hall, Derbyshire, England, about 1757–70.		
	Royal Crescent, Bath, England, 1767–75.	Coade stone invented, 1770s.	
		Circular saw patented in Britain, 1777. Used for processing lumber from 1850s.	
		First iron bridge, Coalbrookdale, Shropshire, 1777–9.	
		Steam engine patented by James Watt, 1782.	
	The Brandenburg Gate, Berlin, Germany, 1789–93.	Henry Cort produces wrought iron by 'puddling', 1784.	
	The Capitol, Washington DC, 1793–1867.	Fireproof floors developed, 1790s.	French Revolution, 1789.
		Cast iron beams and columns used in British factory, 1796.	
		'Roman' cement patented by James Parker, 1796.	
		Civil engineers formed professional society, late 18th century.	
		Scagliola used in interiors, to imitate marble, available from early 19th century.	
19th century		Steam heating installed in textile mill by Boulton and Watt, 1802.	
1810		Gas used for public street lighting in parts of London, 1814.	
1820		Atlantic first crossed by using steam power, 1818.	Final defeat of Napoleon, 1815.
		Terracotta used for building components from 1820s.	
		Cavity walls used from 1820s.	

DATES	BUILDINGS	TECHNOLOGY	EVENTS TIMELINE
		Portland cement patented by Joseph Aspdin, 1824.	
		First public railway opened, Stockton to Darlington line, England, 1825.	
1830		Hot water radiators installed in Westminster Hospital, London, 1830.	
		Concrete rediscovered as a building material, 1830s.	
		Prefabricated buildings made of wood and, later, cast iron, 1830s.	
		Railway stations built from 1830s.	
	London Bridge, London, originally built 1834.	Institute of British Architects, UK, founded, 1834.	
	Concrete house, Swanscombe, Kent, England, 1835.		
	Palace of Westminster, London, 1835–70.		
1840	St George's Hall, Liverpool, England, 1840–54.	Gaslight in homes introduced, 1840s.	
		Societe centrale des architectes francais founded 1843.	
		Excise duty on glass abolished, 1845.	
			Revolutions across Europe, 1848.
1850	All Saints' Church, Margaret Street, London, 1849–59.	Inclined drawing table introduced, 1850s.	
	Crystal Palace, London, 1850–1.	Cylinder method of making flat glass improved to make broad or sheet glass, 1850s.	
		Interchangeability of engineering parts investigated from mid 19th century.	
		Window tax in UK abolished, 1851.	
		Reinforced concrete patented in UK in 1854.	Great Exhibition, London, 1851.
		Electric bulb invented, 1855.	
		American Institute of Architects founded, 1857.	
		Henry Bessemer patents process for manufacture of steel, 1856.	
		First Atlantic cable completed, 1857.	
1860	The University Museum, Oxford, England, 1854–60.	Steam-powered lifts developed by Eli Otis, 1861.	
	Opera House, Paris, 1861–74.	First line opened that was to become London Underground, 1863.	
	Expiatory Church of the Sagrada Familia, Barcelona, Spain, 1863 to the present.		
	Midland Grand Hotel, St Pancras railway station, London, 1865–74.		
	The Mad King's Castle (Schloss Neuschwanstein), Bavaria, Germany, 1869–81.		
1870	Bear Wood, Berkshire, England, 1870.	Typewriter developed, 1870s.	
		Telephone invented, 1876.	
		Edison obtains patent for incandescent lamp, 1879.	
1880		First electric lift built by Werner von Siemens, 1880.	
		Early use of cast-iron frame exploited in Chicago, 1880s.	
		Brick-making machinery available from 1880s.	
		Aluminium becomes cheap structural material, 1880s.	
	The Reichstag, Berlin, 1884–94.	Arches of wrought iron used in Galerie des Machines, Paris, 1889.	International Exhibition, Paris, 1889.
1890		First moving pictures lead to beginning of cinema, 1890s.	
	Tassel House, Brussels, 1892–3.	Steel-reinforced concrete perfected by Hennebique, 1892.	
		Air conditioning systems developed, late 19th/early 20th century.	
	Victoria Railway Terminus, Bombay (Mumbai), India, 1894–6.		
	School of Art, Glasgow, Scotland, 1896.		
	Broadleys, Cartmel, Lancashire[c.f. main text], England, 1898.		
20th century	Carson Pirie Scott Store, Chicago, USA, 1899–1904.	Escalators operated at Paris Exposition, 1900.	
		Photographic blueprint process in general use for reproducing architectural drawings, early 20th century.	
		Space frames developed from early 20th century.	
	Grand Central Station, New York City, USA, 1903–13.	Machine-drawn cylinder glass first produced in USA, 1903.	
	Ritz Hotel, London, 1903–6.		
	The Imperial Austrian Savings Bank, Vienna, 1904.		
	La Samaritaine department store, Paris, 1905–10.		
	The Robie House, Chicago, USA, 1908–9.	Henry Ford devises assembly line for mass production of cars, 1908.	
	AEG Turbine Hall, Berlin, 1909.		
1910	Gamble House, Pasadena, Los Angeles County, USA, 1909.	Neon lighting developed, 1910.	
		Precast concrete, introduced in 1910s, used in much school building and housing after Second World War.	
		First commercial airline service between London and Paris 1919.	First World War, 1914–18.
		Atlantic first crossed by air, 1919.	Russian Revolution, 1917.
1920	Stockholm Public Library, Stockholm, Sweden, 1920–8.	First wireless broadcasting, 1920.	The Bauhaus, Weimar and Dessau, 1919–33.
	Einstein Tower, Potsdam, Germany, 1921.	Schools of Architecture developed in UK, usually attached to existing colleges or universities, from 1900.	
	Church of Notre Dame, Le Raincy, near Paris, 1922–3.	First permanent civil airport building, Königsberg (now Kaliningrad), 1922.	
		Building Research Establishment set up in UK, 1924–5.	

DATES	BUILDINGS	TECHNOLOGY	EVENTS TIMELINE
	Schroeder House, Utrecht, Netherlands, 1924.	First geodesic dome or twenty-planed hemisphere (icosahedral) made in Germany, 1925. *Buckminster Fuller patented same principle, called geodesic domes, 1954.*	
	The Bauhaus, Dessau, Germany, 1925–6.	First control tower, Croydon airport, UK, 1926.	
	Karl Marx Hof, Vienna, 1926–30.	First supermarket: Ralphs stores, Los Angeles, USA, 1928.	
	Maison de Verre, Paris, 1928–32.	Television invented, 1928.	
	Villa Tugendhat, Brno, Czech Republic, 1929–30.		
	Villa Savoye, Poissy, France, 1929–31		Founding of CIAM, spreading Modernism, 1928.
1930	Empire State Building, New York City, USA, 1929–31.	Prestressed concrete developed from 1930s.	Great Depression, 1929–34.
	The Chrysler Building, New York City, USA, 1930.	Introduction of technical pen, 1930s.	
	Rockefeller Center, New York City, USA, 1930–9.	Registration became a mandatory requirement for those practising architecture in Britain, 1931.	
	The Del Rio House, Santa Monica, California, USA, 1931.		
	De la Warr Pavilion, Bexhill-on-Sea, Sussex, England, 1934.		
	Augustus John studio, Freyn Court, Fordingbridge, Hampshire, England, 1934.		
	Gatwick Airport Terminal Building, Sussex, England, 1935–6.	Circular terminal building, Gatwick Airport, with electric telescopic passageways, 1936.	
	Johnson Wax Administration Building, Racine, Wisconsin, USA, 1936–9.		International Style Exhibition at the Museum of Modern Art, New York, 1937.
	Falling Water, Bear Run, Pennsylvania, USA, 1938.		
1940	Dymaxion House, 1945.		Second World War, 1939–45.
	Eames House, Pacific Palisades, Los Angeles, USA, 1945–50.		
	Unité d'Habitation, Marseilles, France, 1946–52.		
1950	Pilgrimage chapel of Notre-Dame du Haut, Ronchamp, France, 1950–4.		
	Crown Hall, Illinois Institute of Technology, Chicago, USA, 1950–6.	Shopping malls developed in the USA, 1950s.	
	Levittown, near Philadelphia, Pennsylvania, USA, 1951–7.	Modular Society founded in UK, 1953.	
	Seagram Building, New York City, USA, 1954–8.	CLASP developed: a building system based on a standard module, 1957.	1951 Festival of Britain. Publication of Le Corbusier's *Le Modulor*.
	The Senate and Congress building, Brasilia, 1957–60.	International Modular Group founded, 1960.	
	Opera House, Sydney, Australia, 1957–73.	Pneumatic structures developed from 1960s.	
1960	Palazzetto dello Sport, Rome, Italy, 1960.		
	Geodesic dome, United States Pavilion, Expo'67, Montreal, Canada, 1967.		Publication of Robert Venturi's *Complexity and Contradiction in Architecture*, 1966.
	Habitat housing, Expo'67, Montreal, Canada, 1967.		
	Trellick Tower, Edenham Street estate, North Kensington, London, 1968–1973.	Ronan Point disaster, east London, 1968.	
	The Byker Wall, Byker Housing Development, Newcastle-upon-Tyne, England, 1969–1980.		
1970	Arcosanti, near Scottsdale, Arizona, USA, from 1970.	CAD introduced as design tool, 1970s.	
	Willis Faber Dumas office, Ipswich, Suffolk, England, 1971–5.		
	The Pompidou Centre, Paris, 1971–7.		
	Olympic Games Stadium, Munich, Germany, 1972.		
			Worldwide energy crisis, 1974.
		ETFE, new cladding material, developed by Hoechst A.G., Germany, 1975.	
	Sainsbury Centre for Visual Arts, University of East Anglia, Norwich, Norfolk, England, 1978.		
	Lloyds Building, London, 1978–86.		
1980	Hong Kong & Shanghai Bank, Hong Kong, 1979–86.		
	Neue Staatsgalerie, Stuttgart, Germany, 1980–3.		
	Institut du Monde Arabe, Paris, 1981–7.		
	Schlumberger Research Centre, Cambridge, England, 1982–6.		
	Richmond Riverside, London, 1988.		
	Waterloo International Terminal, London, 1988–93.		
	Kansai International Airport, Osaka Bay, Japan, 1988–94.		
	Jewish Museum, Berlin, 1989–99.		Fall of Berlin Wall; end of Cold War, 1989.
1990	Dockland Square, Canary Wharf, Tower Hamlets, London, 1991.	Smart glass developed from late 20th century.	
	Jean-Marie Tjibaou Cultural Centre, Nouméa, New Caledonia, 1991–8.		
	Petronas Towers, Kuala Lumpur, 1992–7.		
	Menara Mesiniaga Tower, Kuala Lumpur, 1992.		
	Guggenheim Museum, Bilbao, Spain, 1993–7.		
	Eden Project, St Austell, Cornwall, England, 1996–2001.		
	Commerzbank Headquarters, Frankfurt, Germany, 1997.		Kyoto Protocol on Climate Change, 1997.
	No. 30 St Mary Axe (Swiss Re Headquarters), London, 1997–2004.		
	Bluewater shopping centre, Kent, England, 1998–9.		
	BedZED housing and workspaces, Wallington, England, 1999–2001.		
21st century	Japan Pavilion, Hanover Expo, Hanover, Germany, 2000.		
	House and Office (Straw-bale house), London, 2001.		Destruction of World Trade Center, 2001.
	Downland Gridshell, Weald & Downland Open Air Museum, Chichester, Sussex, England, 2001–2.		

Further Reading

General works

Allen, E. *How Buildings Work: the Natural Order of Architecture* (Oxford, 1995)

Ballantyne, A. *Architecture: a very short introduction* (Oxford, 2002)

Brand, S. *How Buildings Learn: what happens after they're built* rev. ed. (London, 1994)

Ching, F. D. K. *Architecture: form, space and order* 2nd ed. (New York and London, 1996)

Conway, H. & Roenisch, R. *Understanding Architecture: an Introduction to Architecture and Architectural History* (London, 1994)

Giedion, S. *Space, Time and Architecture: the Growth of a New Tradition* 5th ed. (Cambridge, Mass and London, 1967)

Glancey, J. *The Story of Architecture* (London, 2000)

Gorst, T. *The Buildings Around Us* (London, 1995)

Nuttgens, P. *The Story of Architecture* 2nd ed. (London, 1997)

O'Gorman, J. F. *ABC of Architecture* (Philadelphia, 1998)

Architectural theory

Alberti, L. B. *On the Art of Building in Ten Books*, 1485 trans. by Joseph Rykwert, Robert Tavernor, Neil Leach, (Cambridge, Mass and London, 1988)

Bachelard, G. *The Poetics of Space* (Boston, Mass, 1994)

Forty, A. *Words and Buildings: a Vocabulary of Modern Architecture* (London, 2000)

Hays, K. M. ed. *Architecture Theory Since 1968* (Cambridge, Mass and London, 1998)

Hersey, G. L. *The Lost Meaning of Classical Architecture: Speculations on Ornament from Vitruvius to Venturi* (Cambridge, Mass and London, 1988)

Hill, R. *Designs and their Consequences: Architecture and Aesthetics* (New Haven and London, 1999)

Laugier, M. A. *An essay on Architecture*, trans. Wolfgang and Anni Hermann (Los Angeles, 1977)

Le Corbusier *Towards a New Architecture*, trans. John Rodker (London, 1927 and later)

Le Corbusier *The Modulor: a harmonious measure to the human scale universally applicable to architecture and mechanics* (London, 1954)

Palladio, A. *The Four Books of Architecture*, 1570, trans. Robert Tavernor and Richard Schofield (Cambridge, Mass and London, 1997)

Rasmussen, S. E. *Experiencing Architecture* (London, 1959)

Rybczynski, W. *The Look of Architecture* (Oxford, 2001)

Rykwert, J. *The Dancing Column: on Order in Architecture* (Cambridge, Mass and London, 1996)

Shute, J. *The First and Chief Grounds of Architecture: Used in all the Ancient and Famous Monuments* (London, 1563)

Scully, V. *Architecture, the Natural and the Manmade* (New York, 1991)

Venturi, R. *Complexity and Contradiction in Architecture* 2nd ed. (London, 1977)

Vitruvius *Ten Books on Architecture*, trans. Ingrid Rowland. (Cambridge, 1999)

Architectural history

American Buildings and their Architects (5 volumes) (New York and Oxford, 1986)

Braham, A. *The Architecture of the French Enlightenment* (London, 1989)

Crinson, M. & Lubbock, J. *Architecture: Art or Profession?* (Manchester and New York, 1994)

Curtis, W. J. R. *Modern Architecture since 1900* 3rd ed (London, 1996)

Cruickshank, Saint, Frampton and Blundell-Jones, eds. *Sir Banister Fletcher's A History of Architecture* (Oxford, 1996)

Davey, P. *Arts and Crafts Architecture* (London, 1980)

Frampton, K. *Modern Architecture: a Critical History* (London, 1992)

Goodwin, G. *A History of Ottoman Architecture* (London, 1971)

Harvey, J. *The Master Builders: Architecture in the Middle Ages* (London, 1971)

Hillenbrand, R. *Islamic Architecture: Form, Function and Meaning* (Edinburgh, 1994)

Jencks, C. *The New Paradigm in Architecture: the Language of Post-Modernism* (New Haven and London, 2002)

Kostof, S. *A History of Architecture: Settings and Rituals* (Oxford, 1995)

Michell, G. ed. *Architecture of the Islamic world: Its History and Social Meaning* (London, 1978)

Murray, P. *Renaissance Architecture* (London, 1986)

Naylor, G. *The Bauhaus reassessed: sources and design theory* (London, 1985)

Onians, J. *Bearers of Meaning: the Classical Orders in Antiquity, the Middle Ages, and the Renaissance* (Cambridge, 1988)

Pearman, H. *Contemporary World Architecture* (London, 1998)

Pevsner, N. *An Outline of European Architecture* 7th rev ed. (Harmondsworth, 1963)

Pevsner, N. *A History of Building Types* (London, 1986)

Platt, C. *The Architecture of Medieval Britain: a Social History* (New Haven and London, 1990)

Saint, A. *The Image of the Architect* (London and New Haven, 1983)

Steele, J. *Architecture Today* (London, 1997)

Sutton, I. *Western Architecture: a Survey* (London, 1999)

Summerson, Sir J. *The Classical Language of Architecture* (London, 1980)

Tadgell, C. *The History of Architecture in India: from the Dawn of Civilization to the End of the Raj* (London, 1991)

Tafuri, M. & Dal Co, F. *Modern Architecture* (London, 1986)

Tzonis, A. & Lefevre, L. *Classical Architecture: the poetics of order* (Cambridge, Mass and London, 1986)

Vale, L. J. *Architecture, Power and National Identity* (New Haven and London, 1992)

Watkin, D. *The Rise of Architectural History* (London, 1980)

Watkin, D. *English Architecture: a Concise History* (London, 2001)

Watkin, D. *A History of Western Architecture* (London, 2000)

Wilson Jones, M. *Principles of Roman Architecture* (New Haven and London, 2000)

See also architecture books in Thames & Hudson 'World of Art' series and Yale University Press 'Pelican History of Art' series.

Biographies and encyclopaedias

British Architectural Library. *Royal Institute of British Architects Directory of British Architects, 1834–1914* (London, 2001)

Ching, F. D. K. *A Visual Dictionary of Architecture* (New York and London, 1995)

Colvin, H. M. *A Biographical Dictionary of British Architects 1660–1840* (New Haven and London, 1995)

Curl, J. S. *Encyclopaedia of Architectural Terms* (London, 1993)

Emanuel, M. ed. *Contemporary Architects* 3rd ed. (New York and London, 1994)

Fleming, Honour and Pevsner. *The Penguin Dictionary of Architecture and Landscape Architecture* 5th ed. (London, 1998)

Gray, A. S. *Edwardian Architecture: a Biographical Dictionary* (London, 1985)

Harris, J. & Lever, J. *Illustrated Dictionary of Architecture 800–1914* 2nd ed. (London, 1993)

McDonald, R. *Illustrated Building Glossary* (Oxford, 1999)

Magnano Lampugniani, V. ed. *The Thames and Hudson Encyclopaedia of Twentieth Century Architecture* (London, 1986)

Oliver, P. ed. *Encyclopaedia of Vernacular Architecture of the World* (Oxford, 1995)

Placzek, A. K. ed. *Macmillan Encyclopaedia of Architects* (London, 1982)

Stein, J. S. *Construction Glossary: an Encyclopaedic Reference and Manual* (New York, 1980)

Technology and structure

Banham, R. *The Architecture of the Well-Tempered Environment* (London, 1984)

Berger, H. *Light structures: structures of light: the art and engineering of tensile architecture* (Basle, 1996)

Bowyer, J. *History of Building* 2nd ed. (Builth Wells, 1993)

Brunskill, R. W. *Timber Building in Britain* 2nd ed.

(London, 1994)

Brunskill, R. W. *Vernacular Architecture: an Illustrated Handbook* 4th ed. (London, 2000)

Campbell, J. W. P. & Pryce, W. *Brick: a World History* (London, 2003)

Clifton-Taylor, A. *English Stone Building* new ed. (London, 1994)

Clifton-Taylor, A. *The Pattern of English Building* 4th ed. (London, 1987)

Collins, P. *Concrete: the Vision of a New Architecture: a Study of Auguste Perret and his Precursors* (London, 1959)

Cowan, H. *The Master Builders: a History of Structural and Environmental Design from Ancient Egypt to the Nineteenth Century* (New York, 1977)

Edwards, B. *Rough Guide to Sustainability* (London, 2001)

Elliott, C. D. *Technics and Architecture: the Development of Materials and Systems for Buildings* (Cambridge, Mass and London, 1992)

Fitchen, J. *Building construction before mechanization* (Cambridge, Mass and London, 1986)

Guedes, P. *The Macmillan Encyclopaedia of Architecture and Technological Change* (London, 1979)

Hawkes, D. & Forster, W. *Architecture, Engineering and Environment* (London, 2002)

Hix, J. *The Glasshouse* (London, 1996)

Kronenburg, R. H. *Houses in Motion: the Genesis, History and Development of Portable Architecture* (London, 2002)

Leach, N. ed. *Designing for a digital world* (Chichester, 2002)

Levy, M. & Salvadori, M. *Why buildings fall down: how structures fail* (New York and London, 1992)

Lloyd-Jones, D. *Architecture and the Environment: Bioclimatic Building Design* (London, 1998)

Macdonald, A. J. *Structure and architecture* (Oxford, 2001)

Mainstone, R. *Developments in structural form* 2nd ed. (Oxford, 1998)

Mark, R. ed. *Architectural technology up to the Scientific Revolution: the Art and Structure of Large-Scale Buildings* (Cambridge, Mass, 1993)

Morriss, R. K. *The Archaeology of Buildings* (Stroud, 2000)

Robbin, T. *Engineering a New Architecture* (New Haven and London, 1996)

Rudlin, D. *Building the 21st century Home: the Sustainable Urban Neighbourhood* (Oxford, 1999)

Rudofsky, B. *The Prodigious Builders* (London, 1977)

Salvadori, M. & Heller, R. *Structure in Architecture: the Building of Buildings* 3rd ed (1986)

Salvadori, M. *Building: the Fight against Gravity* (New York, 1979)

Salzman, L. F. *Building in England down to 1540, a Documentary History* (Oxford, 1952)

Strike, J. *Construction into Design: the Influence of New Methods of Construction on Architectural Design 1690–1990* (Oxford, 1991)

Wigginton, M. *Glass in Architecture* (London, 1996)

Town planning & built environment

Ayres, J. *Building the Georgian City* (London, 1998)

Braunfels, W. *Urban Design in Western Europe: Regime and Architecture 900-1900* (Chicago, 1988)

Creese, W. L. *The search for environment: the garden city, before and after* (Baltimore and London, 1992)

Davis, M. *City of Quartz: Excavating the Future in Los Angeles* (London, 1990)

Eaton, R. *Ideal Cities: Utopianism and the (Un)built Environment* (London, 2001)

Essex Planning Officers Association. *Essex Design Guide for Residential and Mixed Used Areas* new ed. (Chelmsford, 1997)

Girouard, M. *Cities and People; a Social and Architectural History* (New Haven and London, 1985)

Girouard, M. *The English Town* (New Haven and London, 1990)

Hall, Sir P. *Cities of Tomorrow: an Intellectual history of Urban Planning and Design in the Twentieth Century* 3rd edition (Oxford, 2002)

Hall, Sir P. *Cities in Civilisation. Culture, Innovation and Urban Order* (London, 1998)

Howard, E. *Garden Cities of Tomorrow* (Eastbourne, 1985)

Jacob, J. *The Death and Life of Great American Cities* (New York, 1961)

Kostof, S. *The City Assembled: the Elements of Urban Form through History* (London, 1992)

Kostof, S. *The City Shaped: Urban Patterns and Meanings through History* (London, 1991)

Le Corbusier. *The City of Tomorrow and its Planning* (London, 1971)

LeGates, R. T. & Stout F. eds. *The City Reader* 3rd ed (London, 2003)

Lynch, K. *A Theory of Good City Form* (Cambridge, Mass, 1981)

Mumford, L. *The City in History: its Origins, its Transformations and its Prospects* (London, 1961)

Olsen, D. J. *The city as a work of art: London, Paris, Vienna* (New Haven and London, 1986)

Rasmussen, S. E. *London: the Unique City* (Cambridge, Mass, 1982)

Ravetz, A. *Council Housing and Culture: the History of a Social Experiment* (London, 2001)

Rykwert, J. *The Idea of a Town: an Anthropology of Urban Form in Rome, Italy and the Ancient World* (Cambridge, Mass and London, 1988)

Rykwert, J. *The Seduction of Place: the City in the Twenty-first Century* (London, 2000)

Summerson, Sir J. *Georgian London* rev. ed. (London, 2003)

Venturi, Scott Brown and Izenour. *Learning from Las Vegas* (Cambridge, Mass, 1972)

INDEX